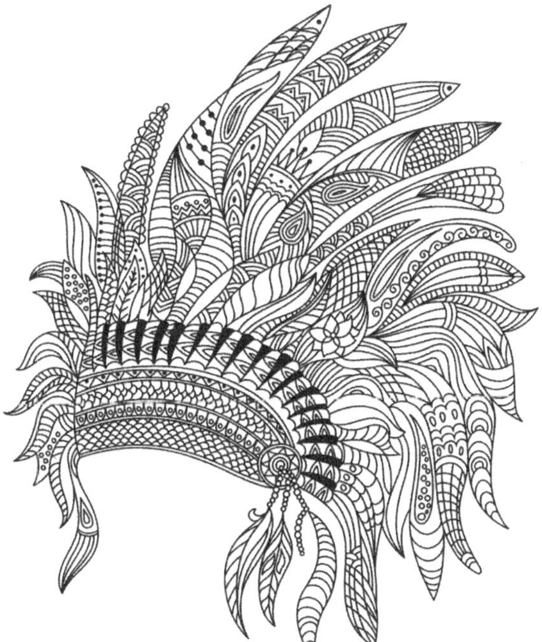

NATIVE AMERICAN

Adult Coloring Book

DYLANNA
Press

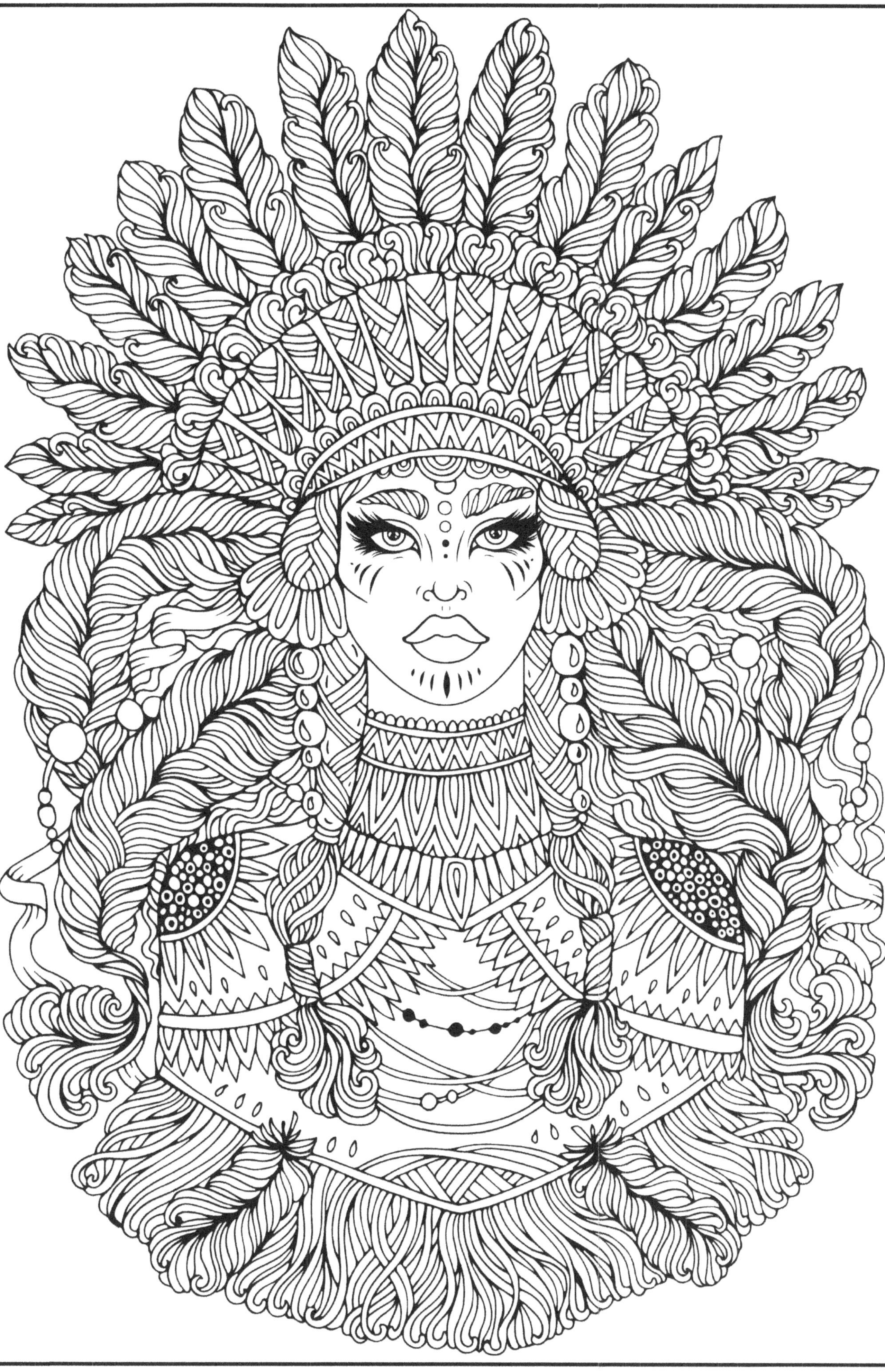

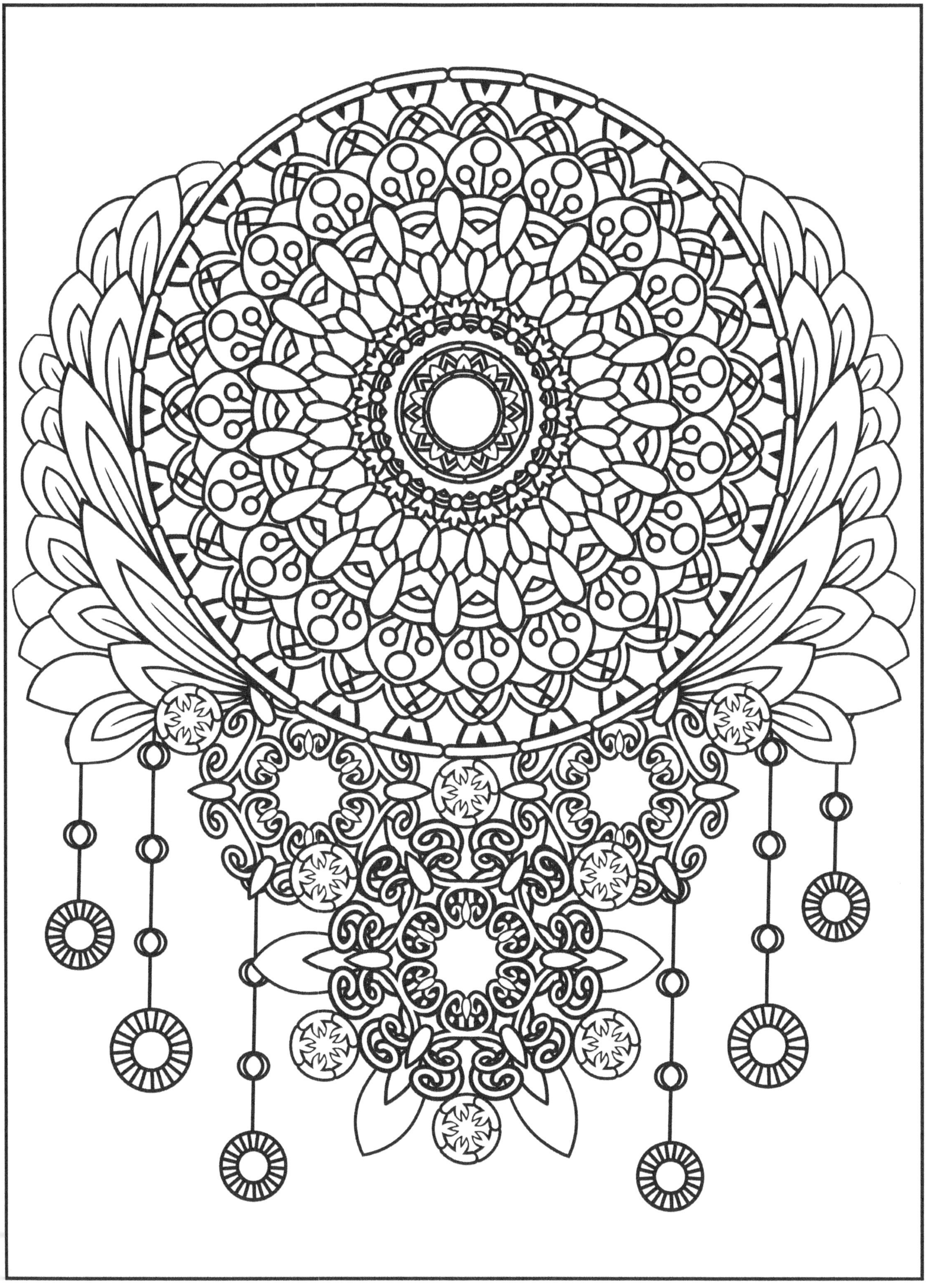

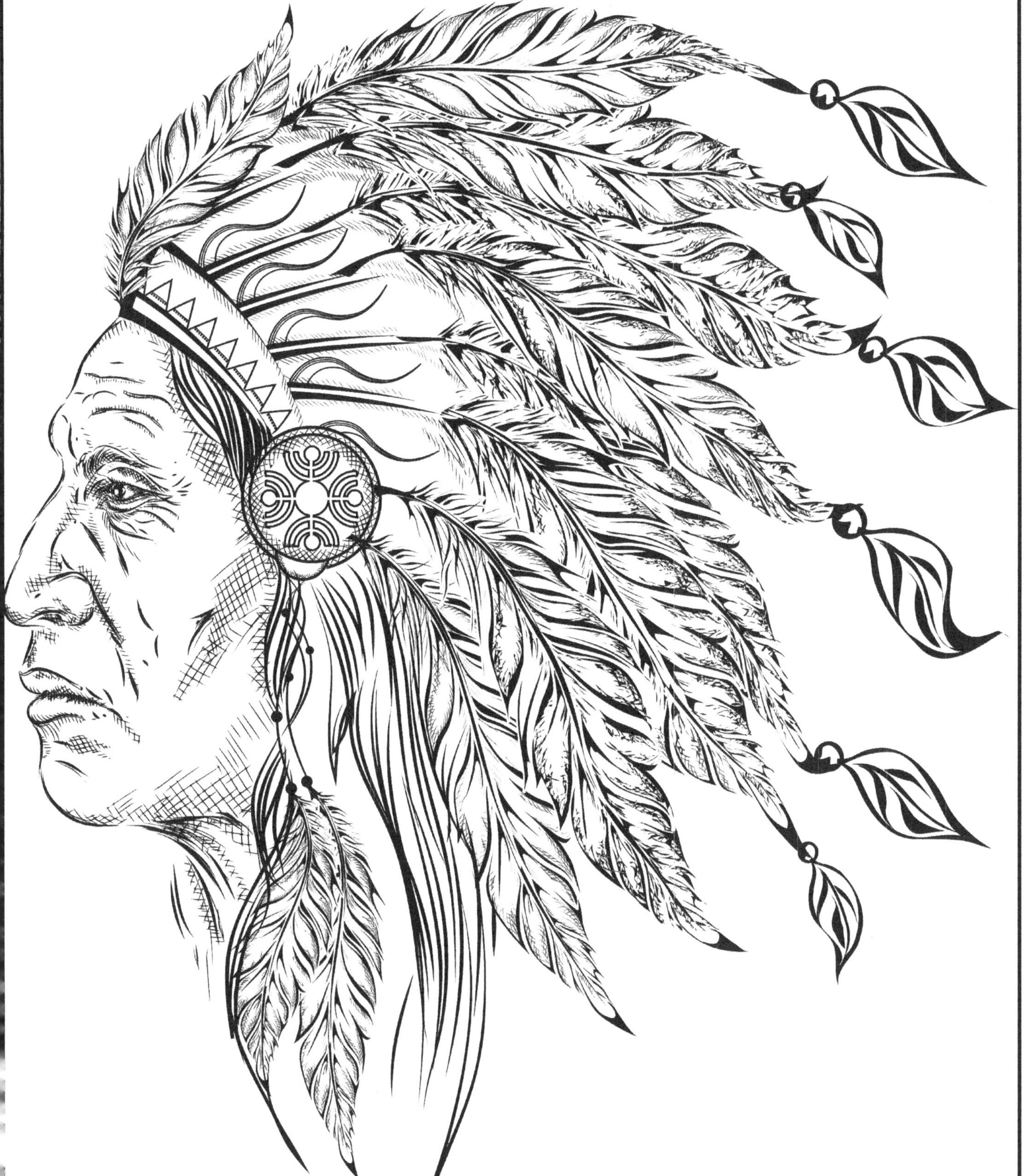

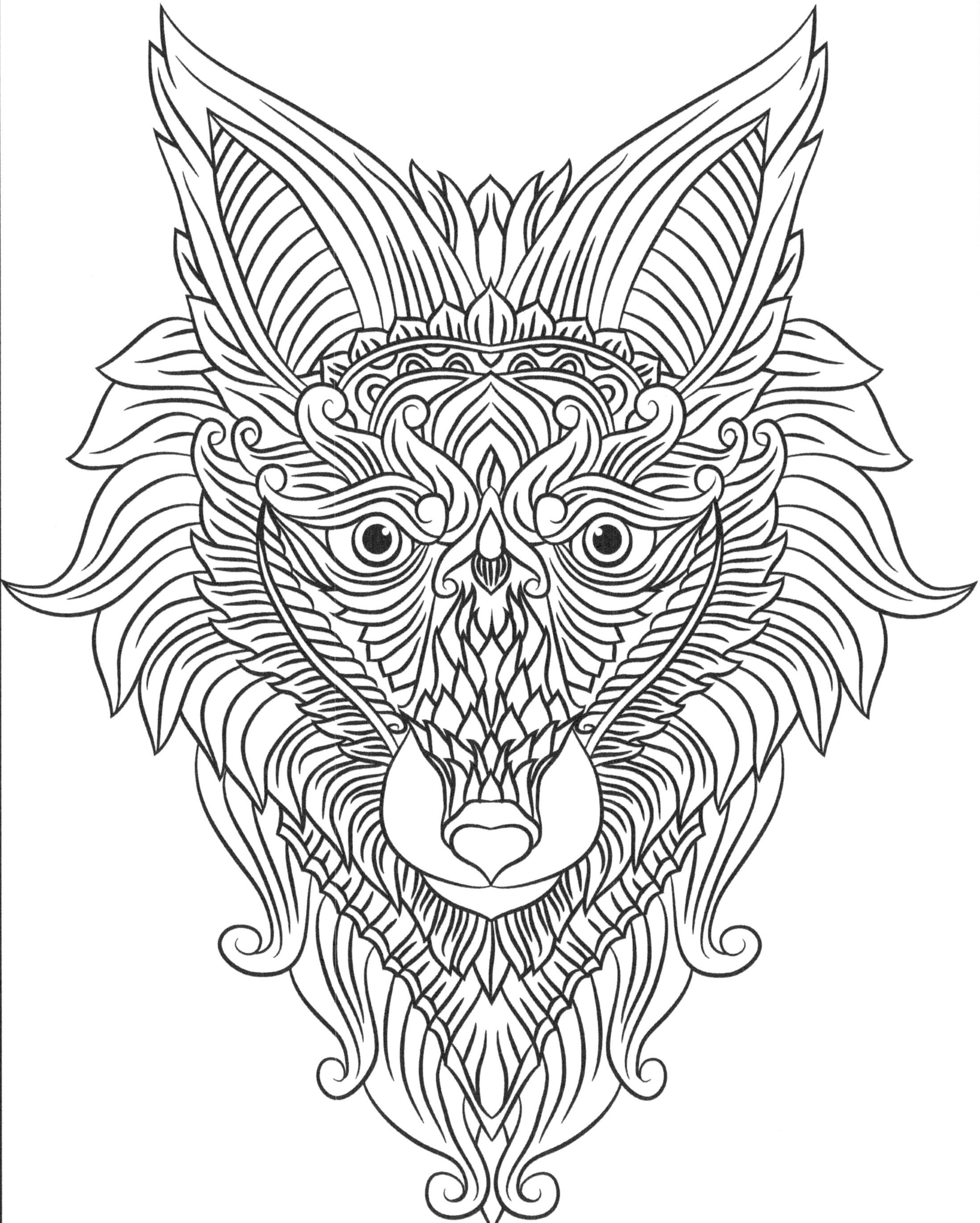

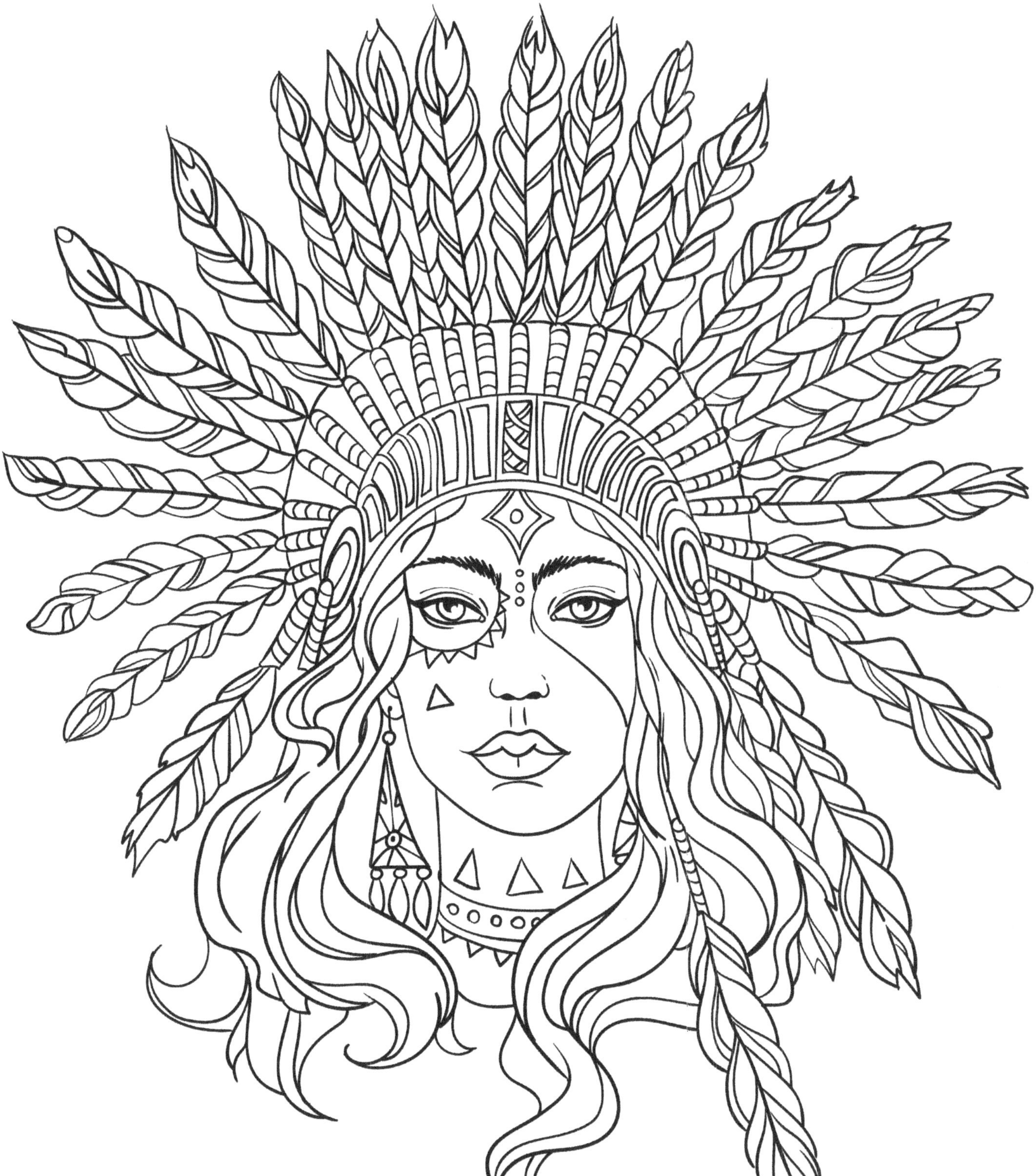

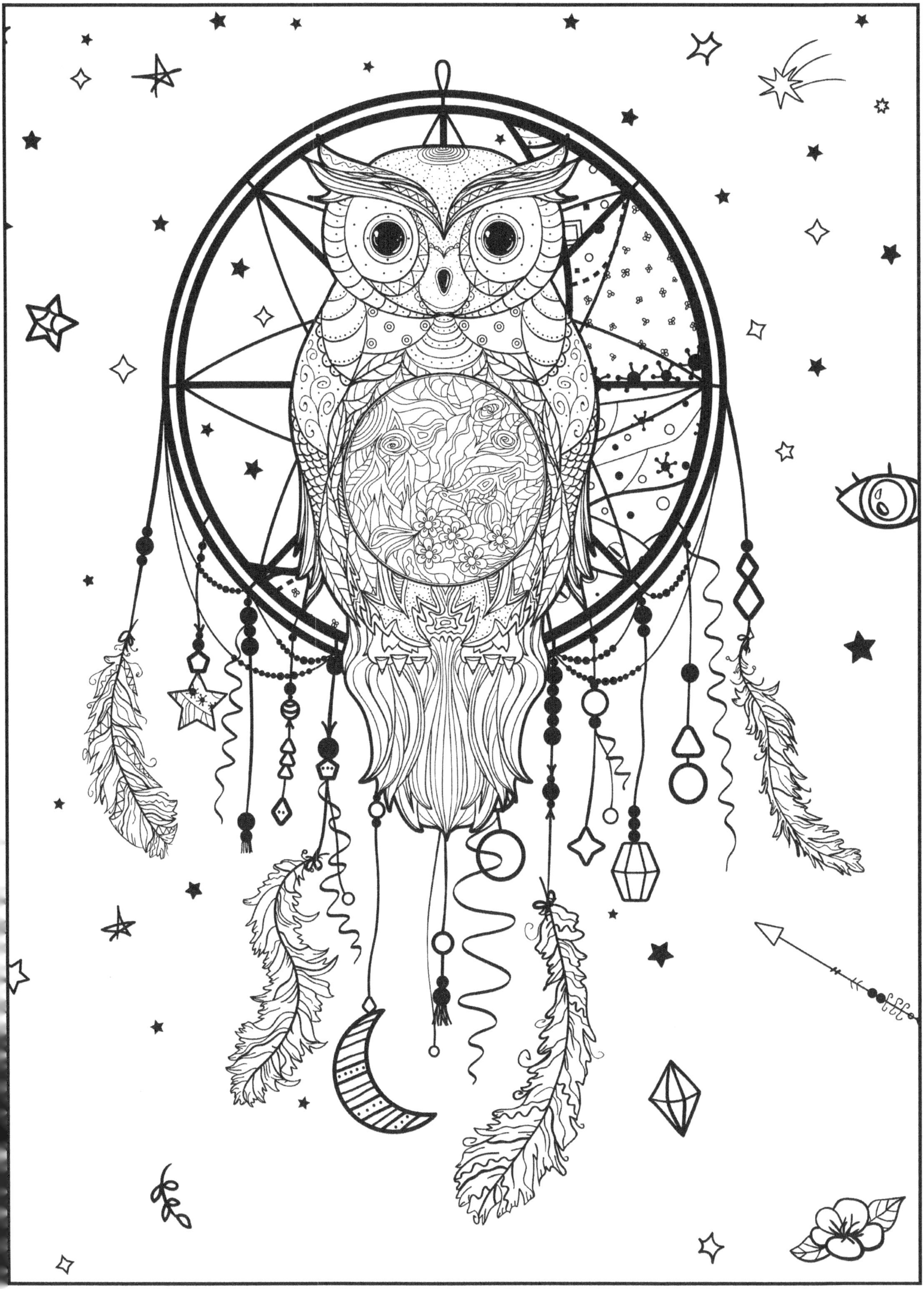

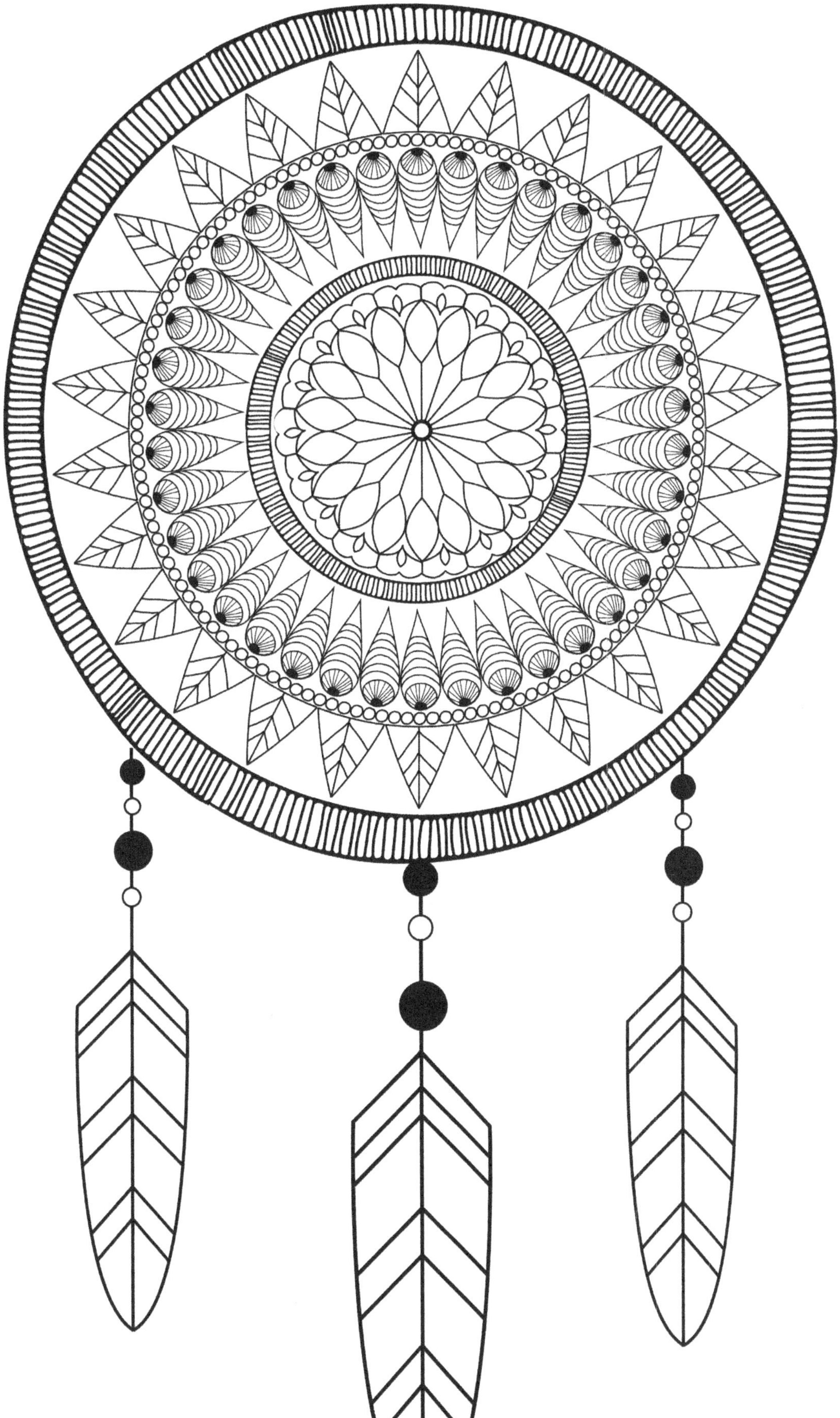

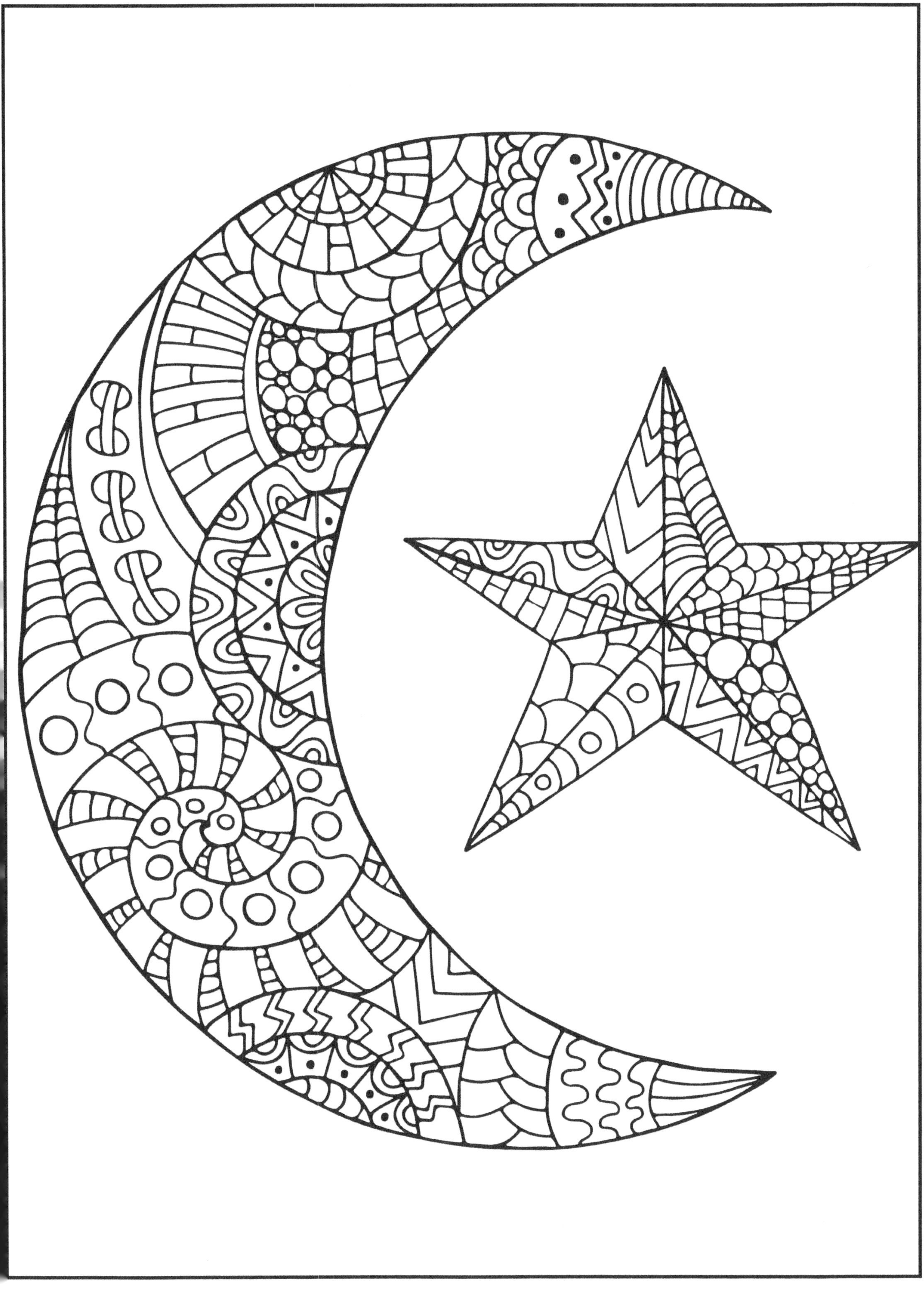

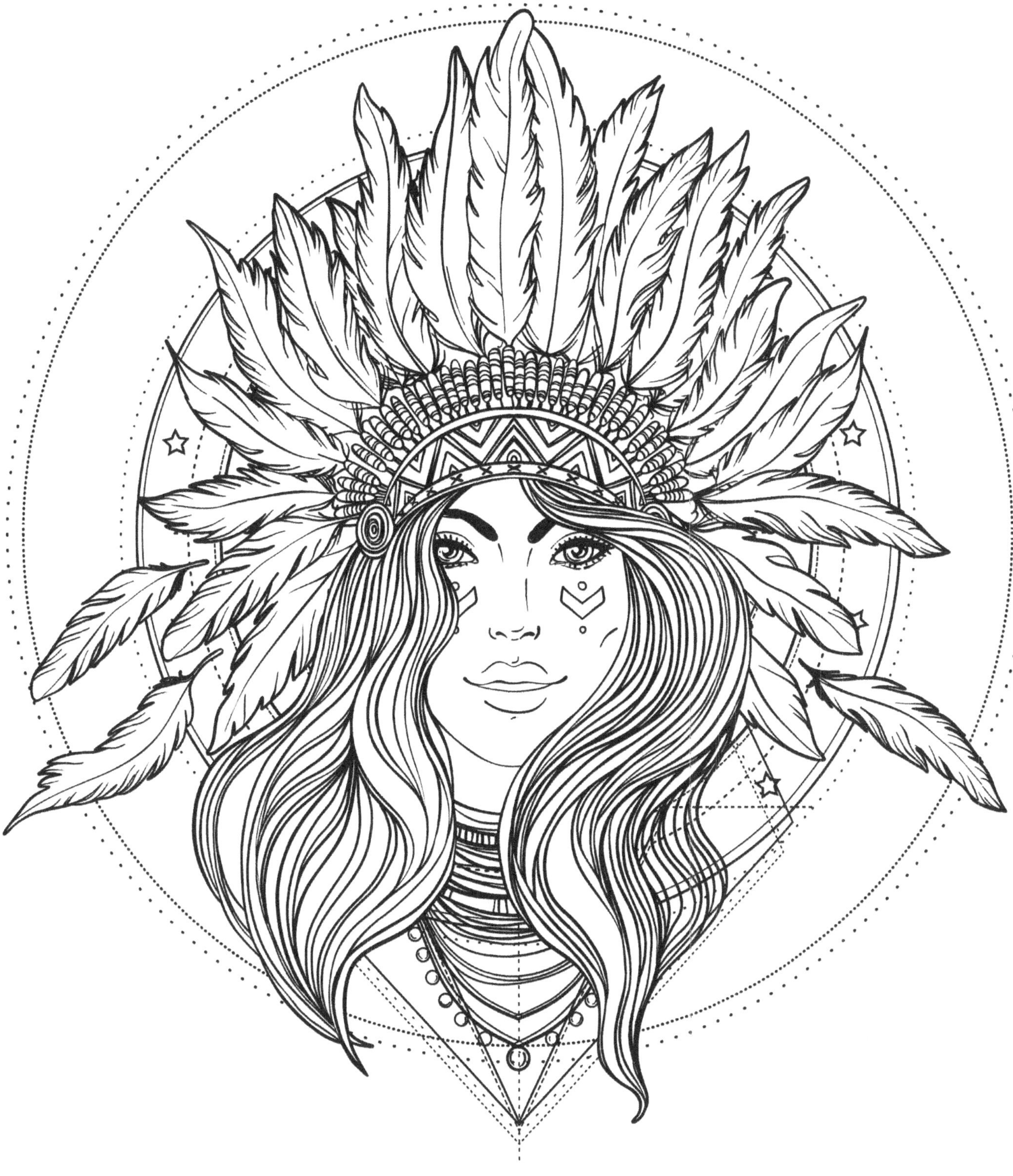

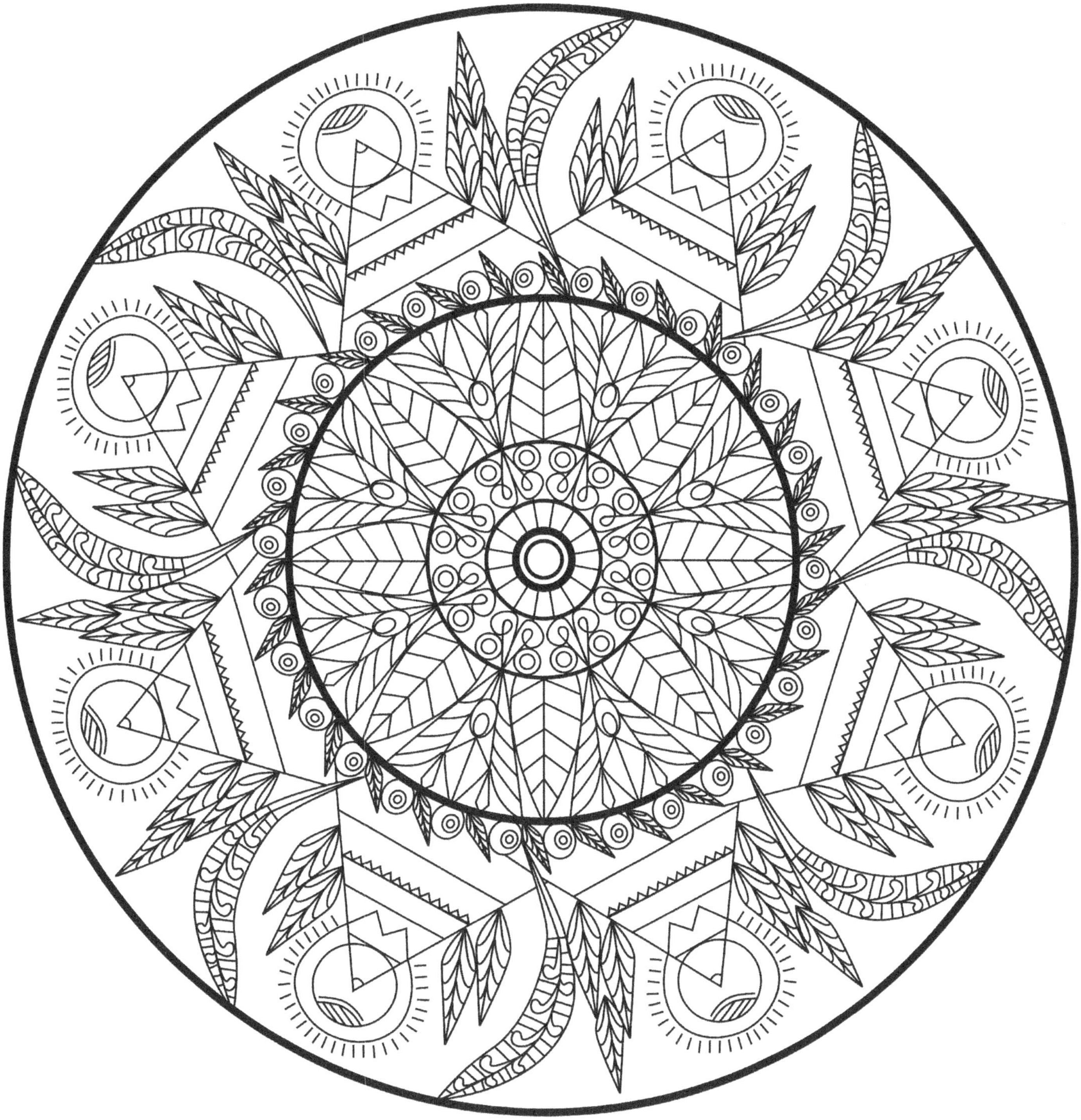

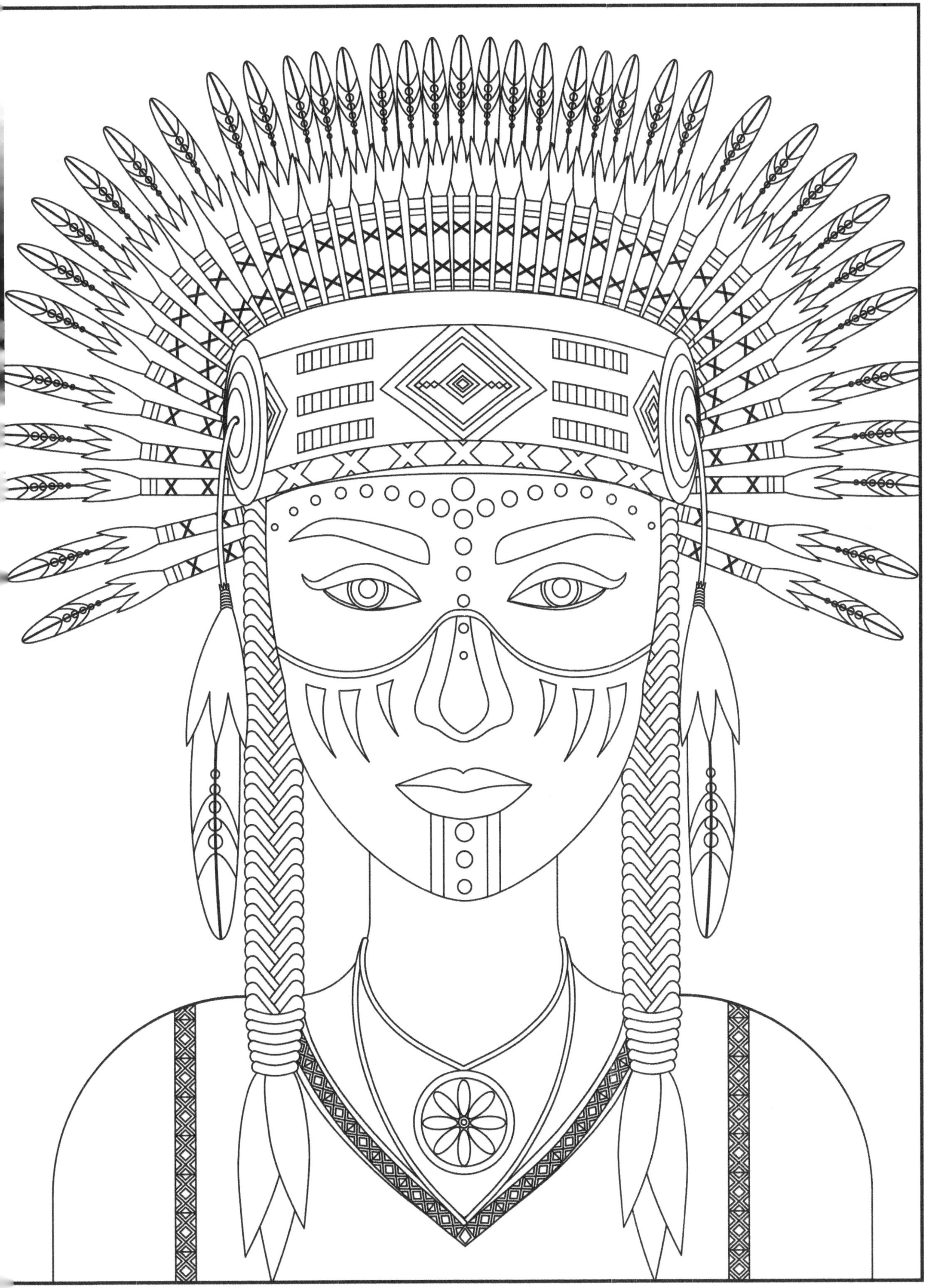

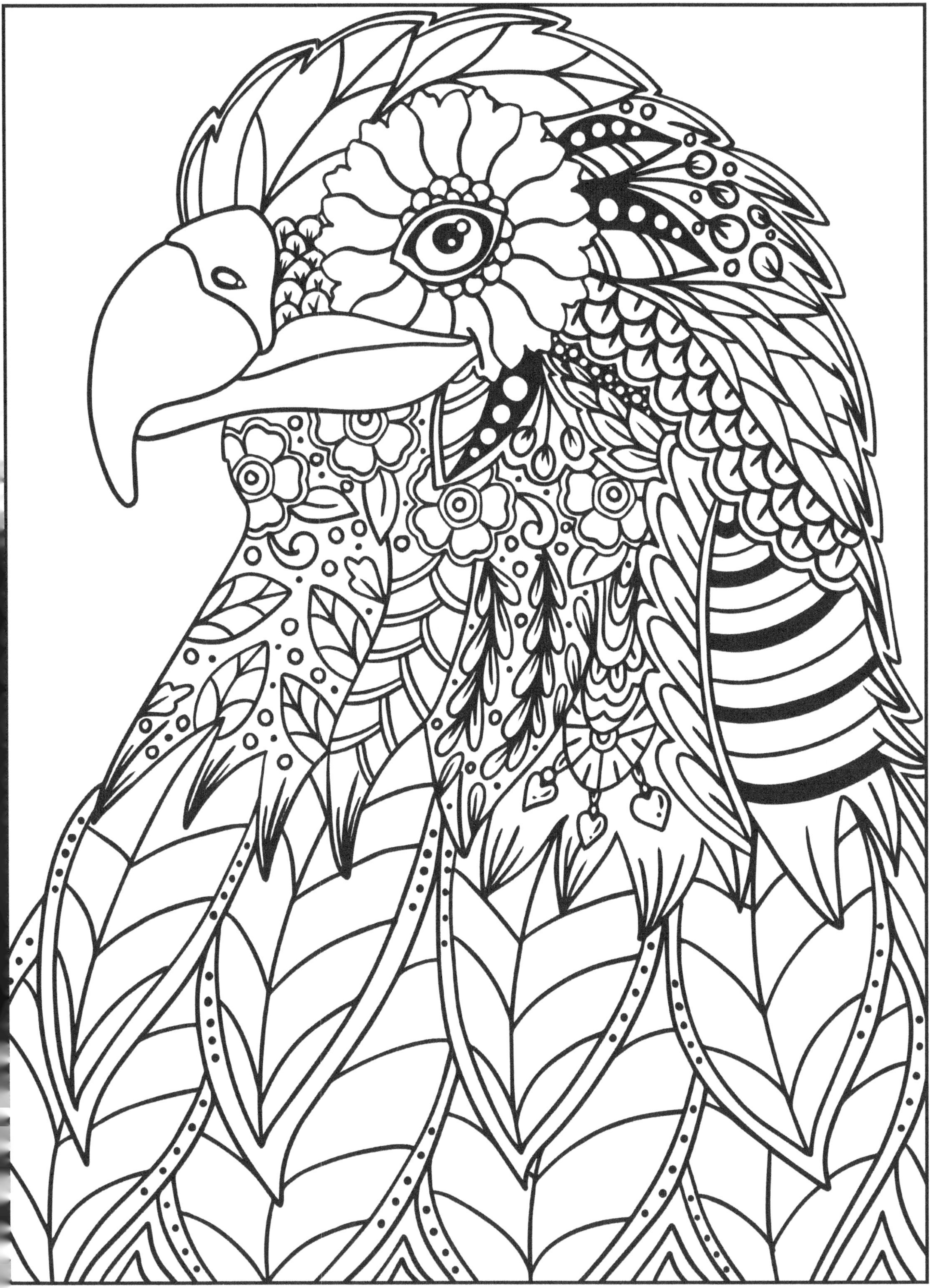

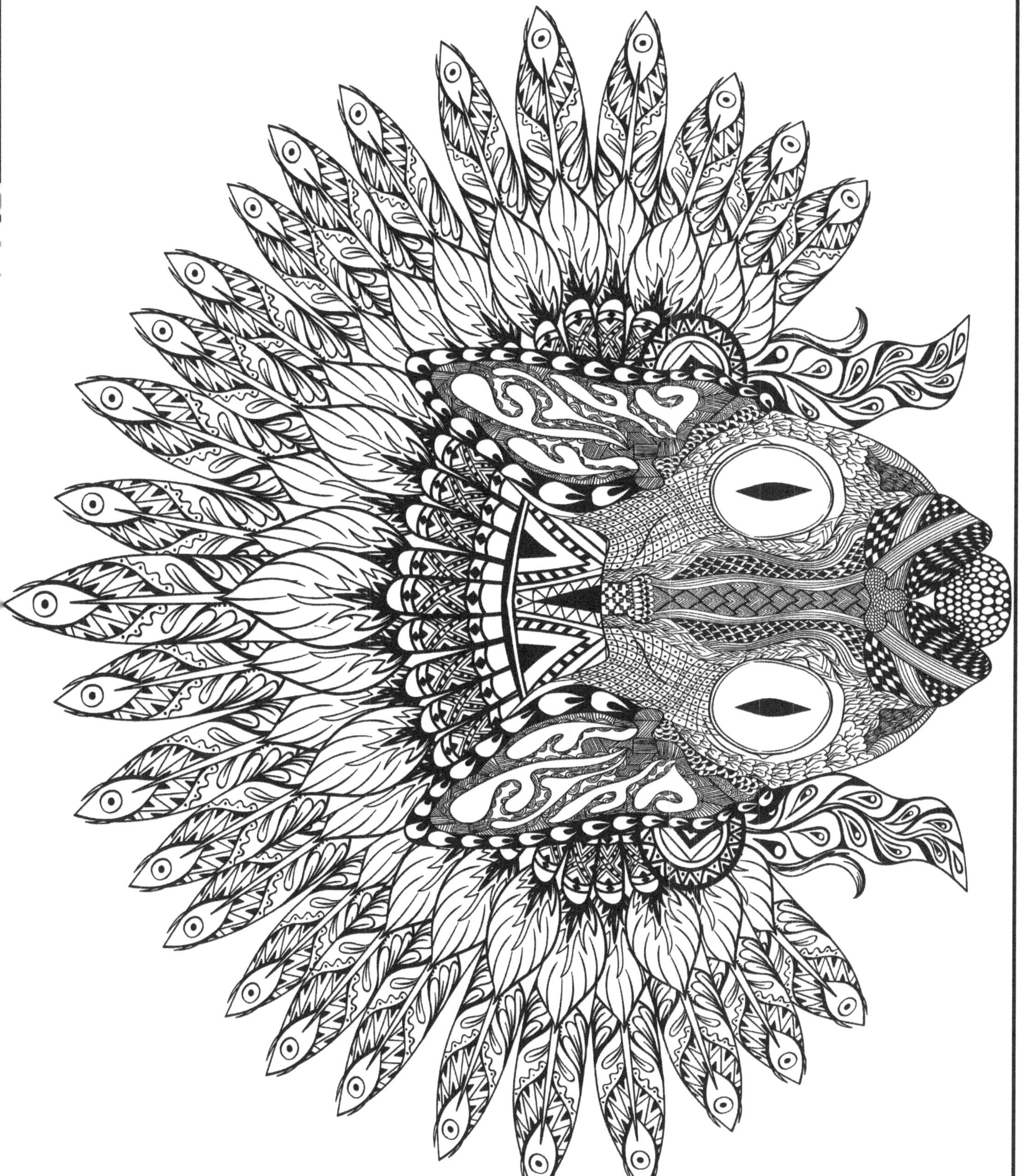

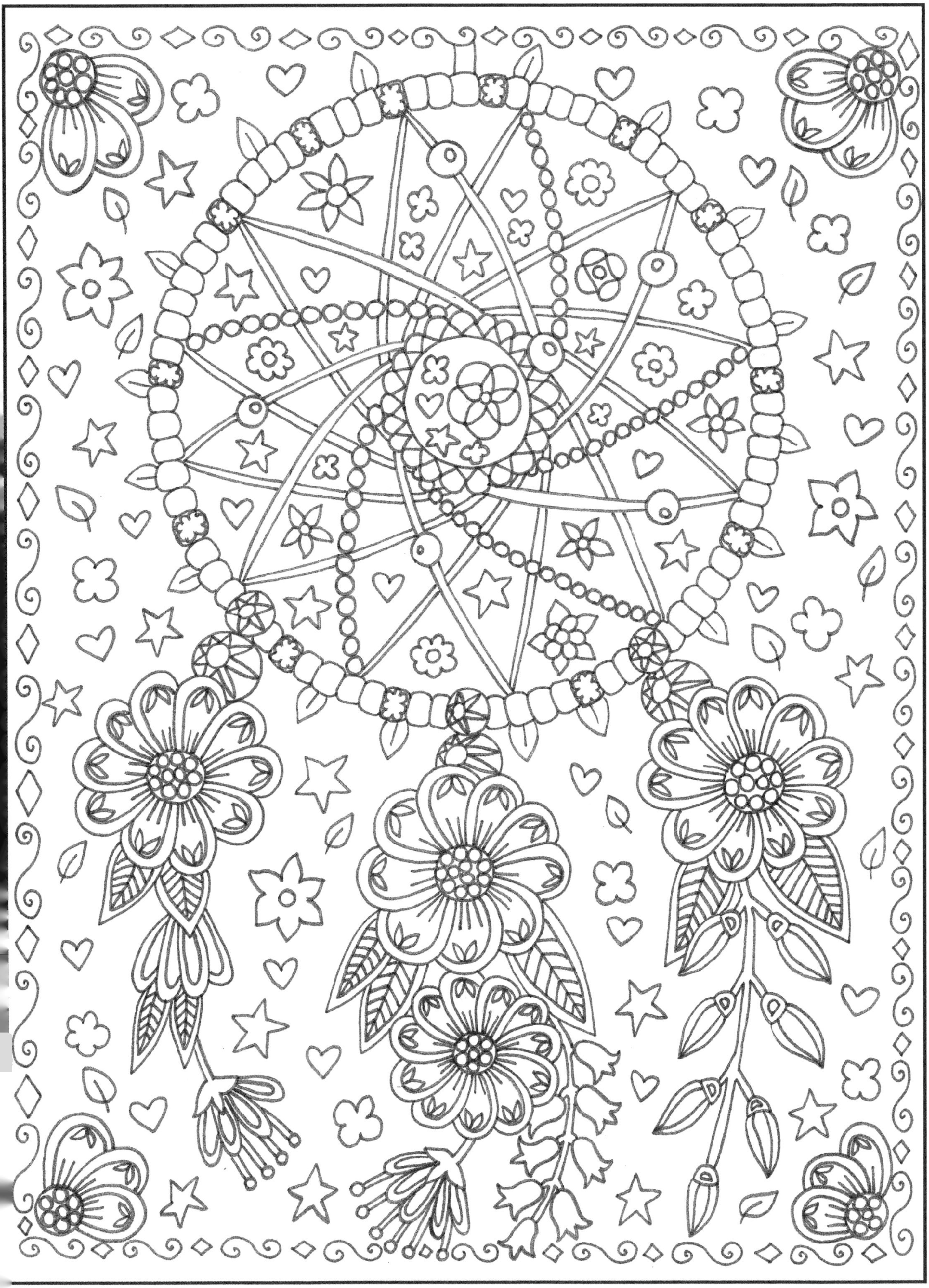

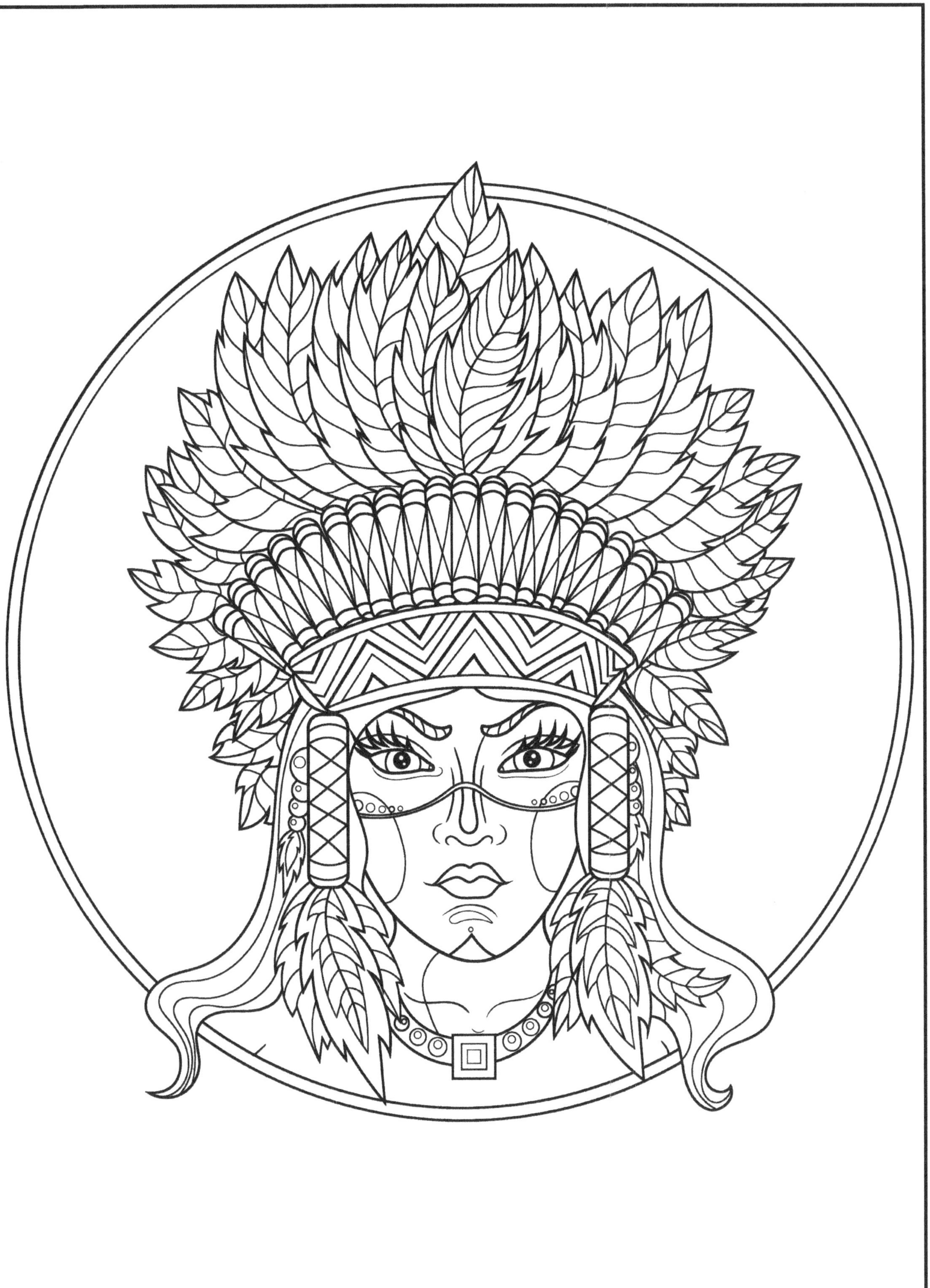

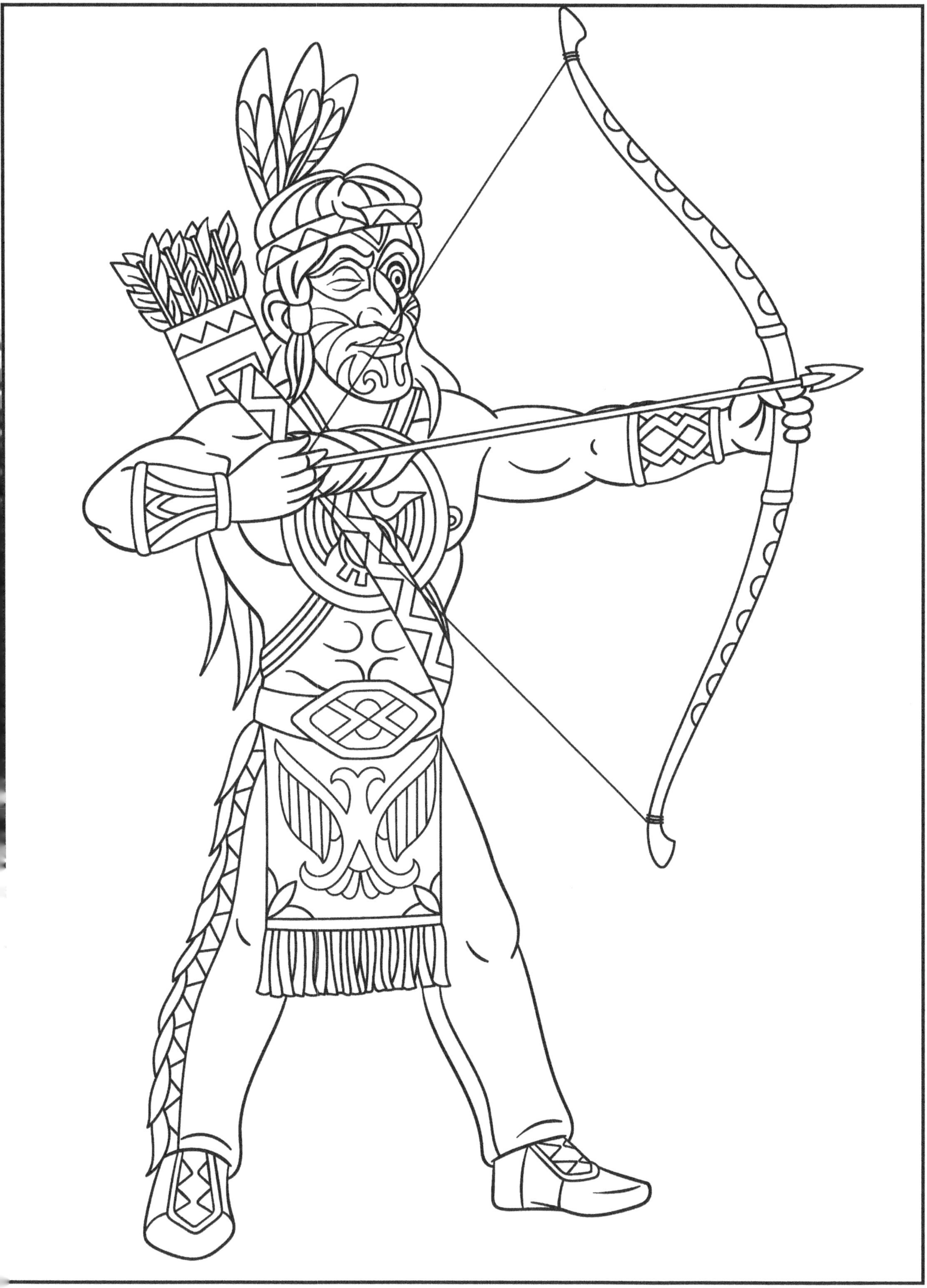

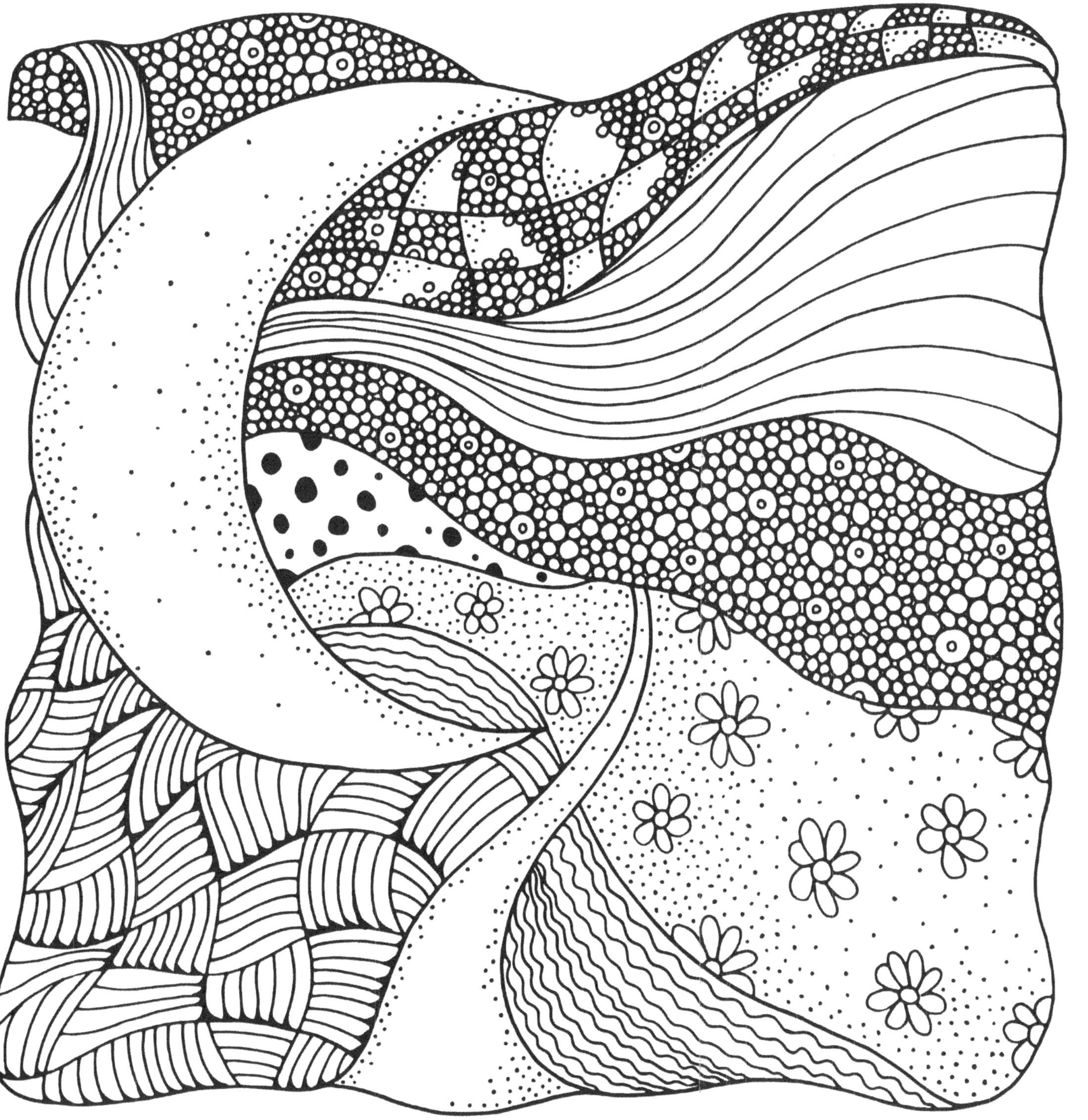

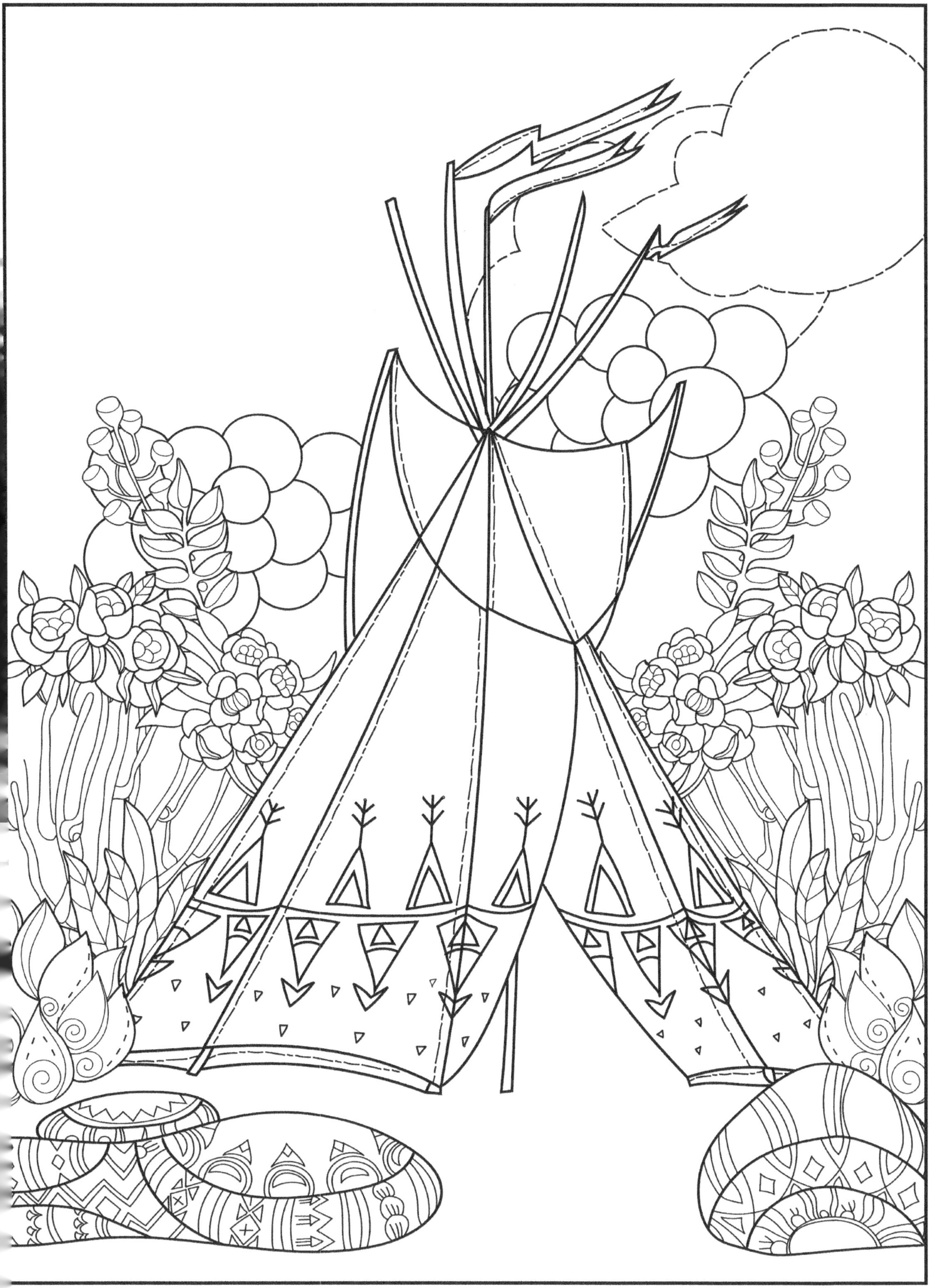

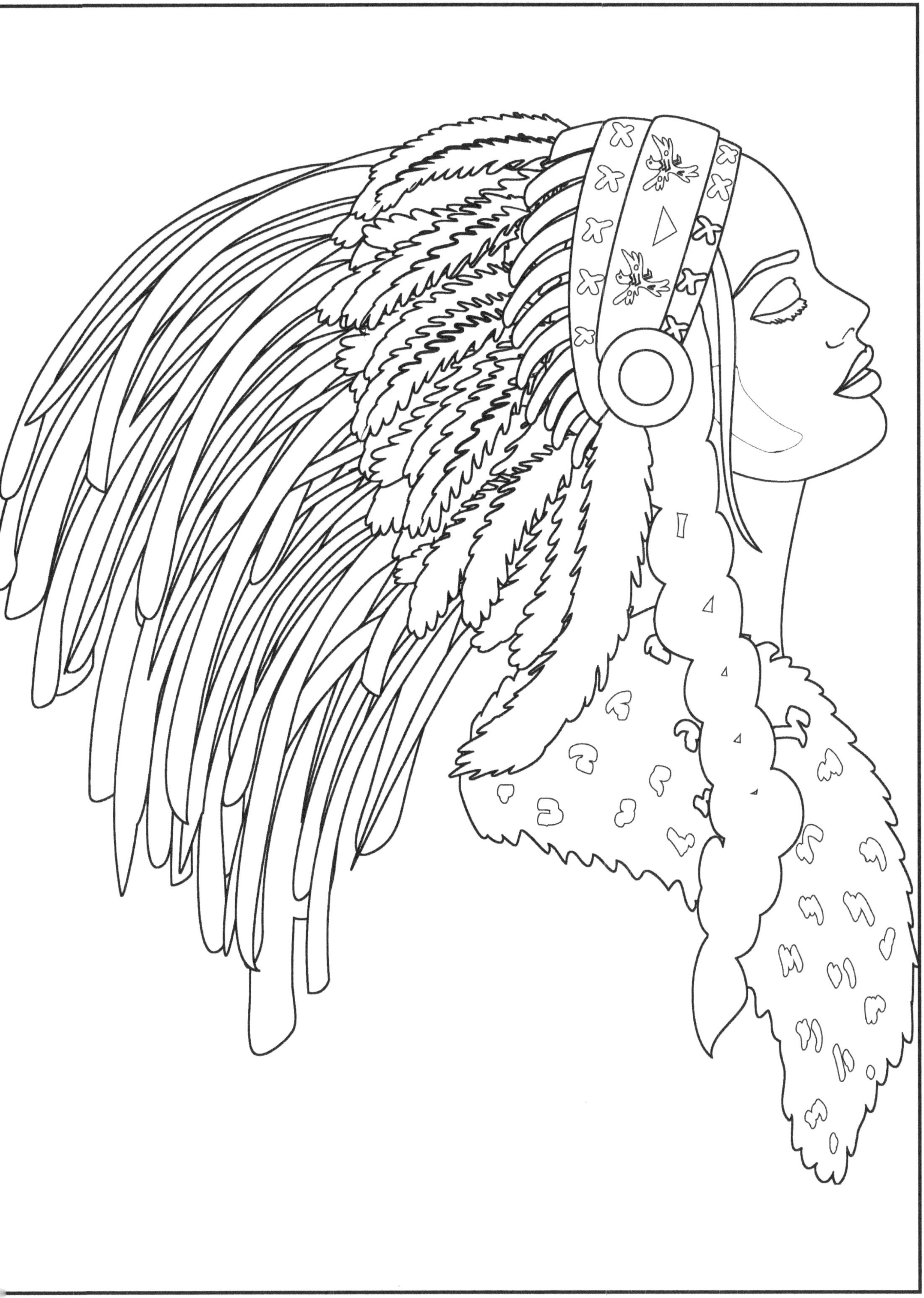

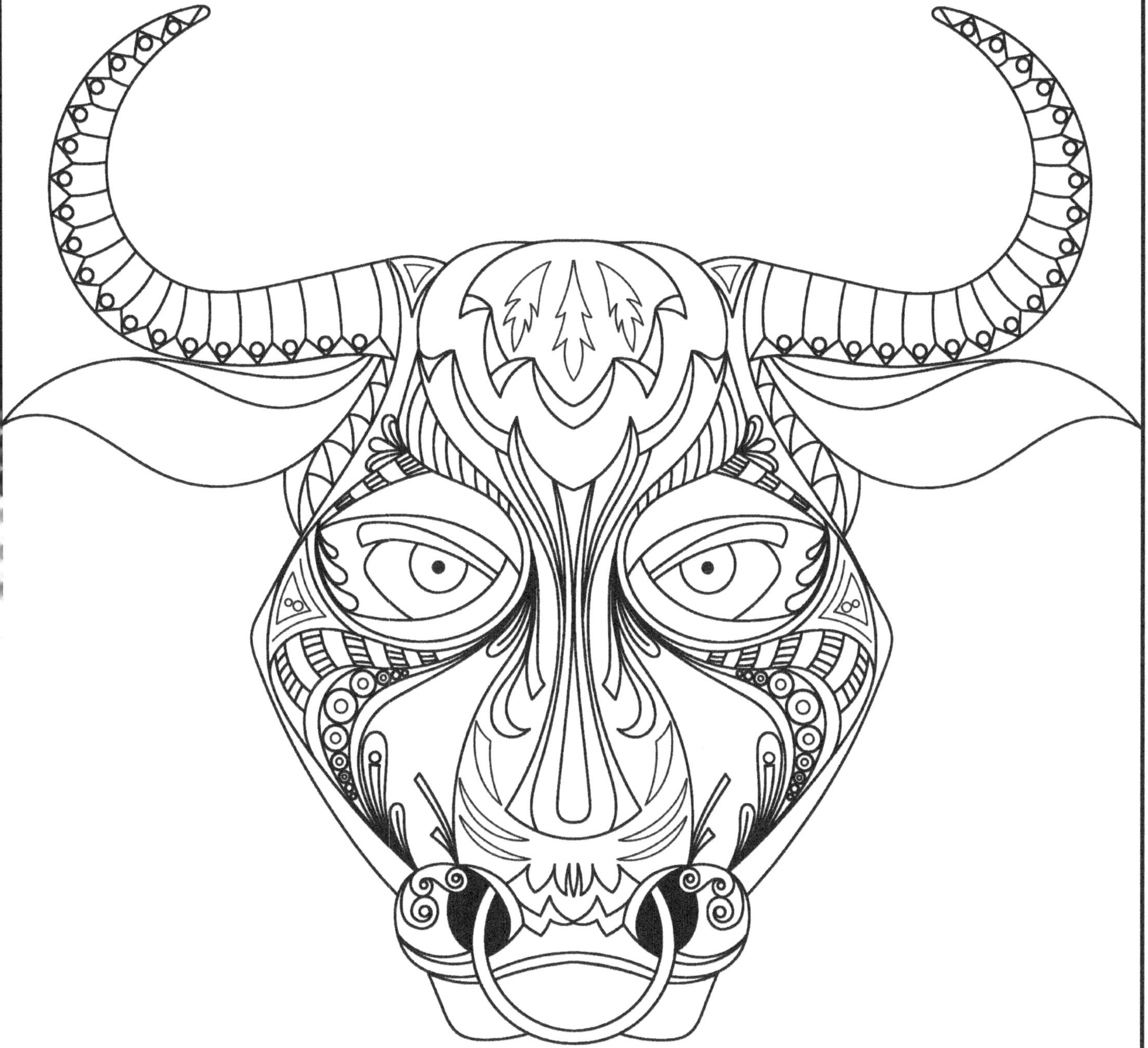

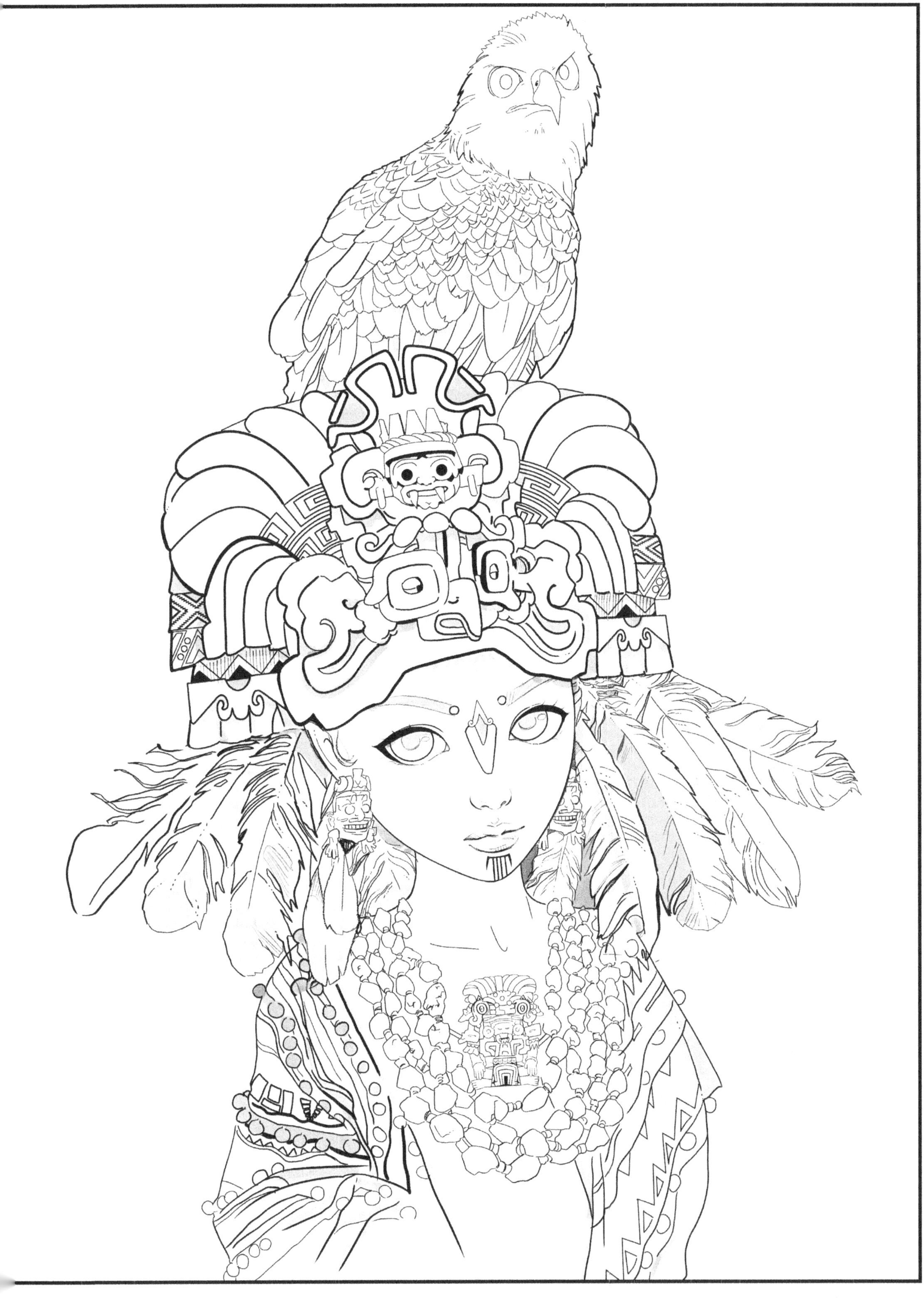

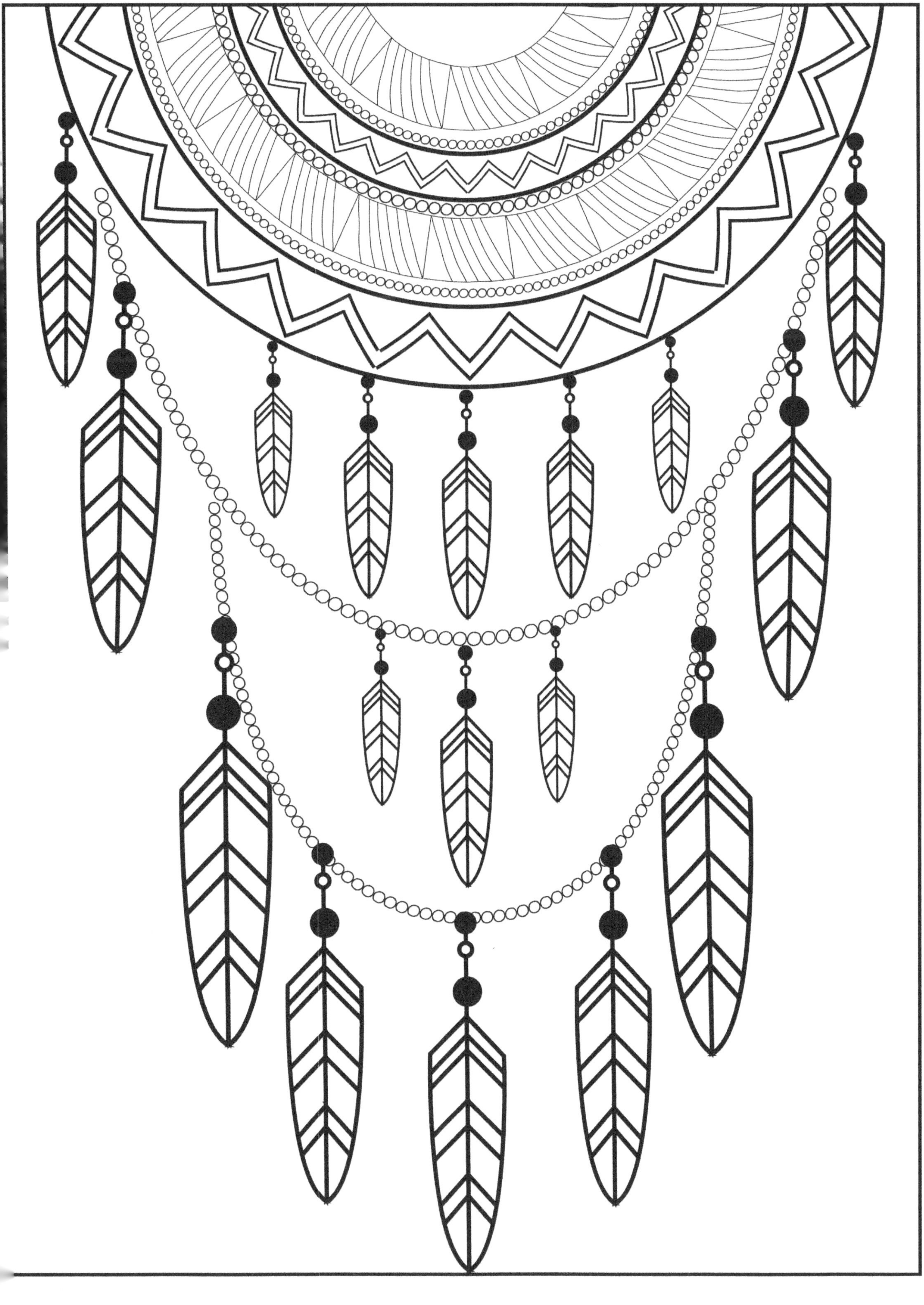

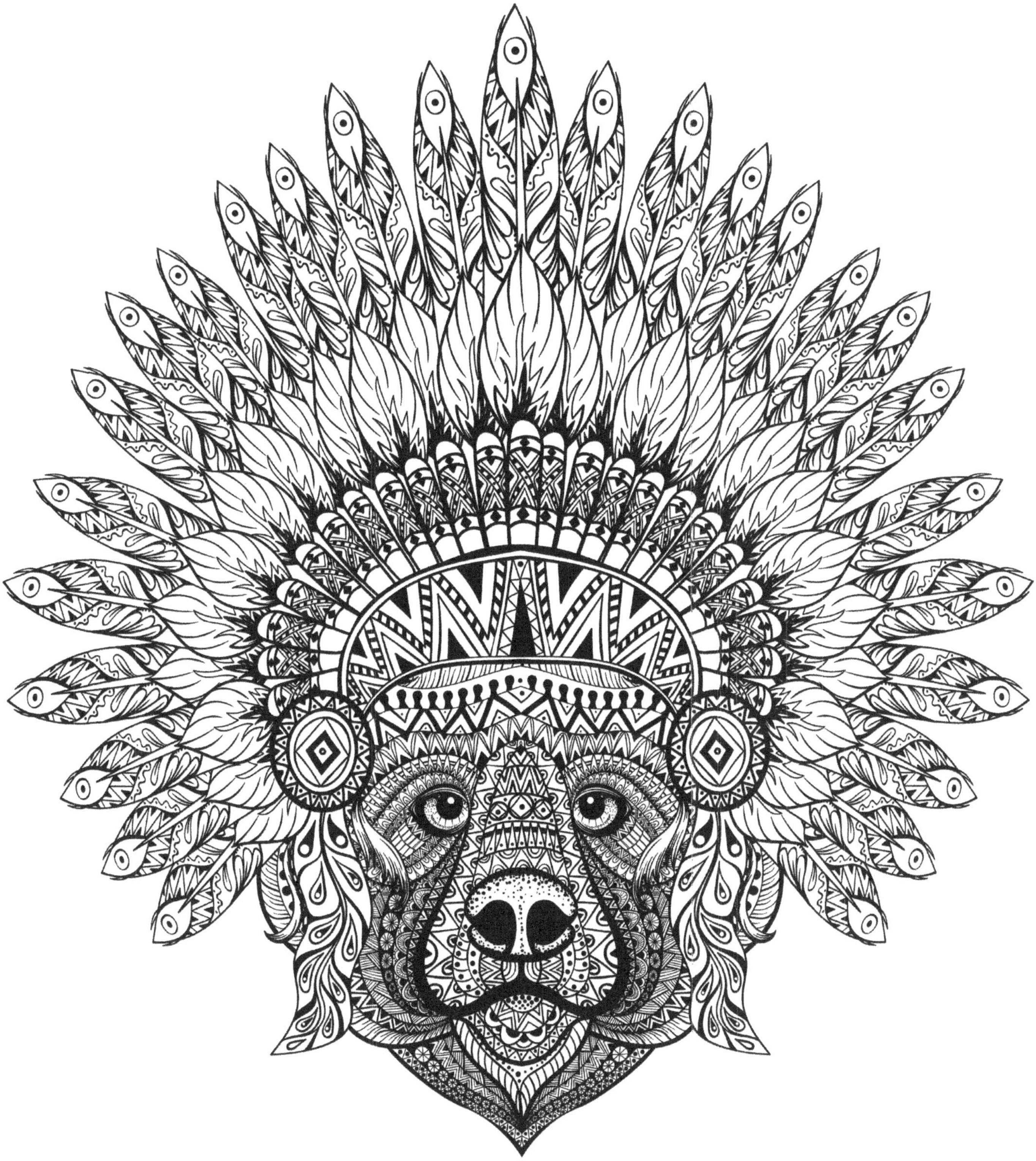

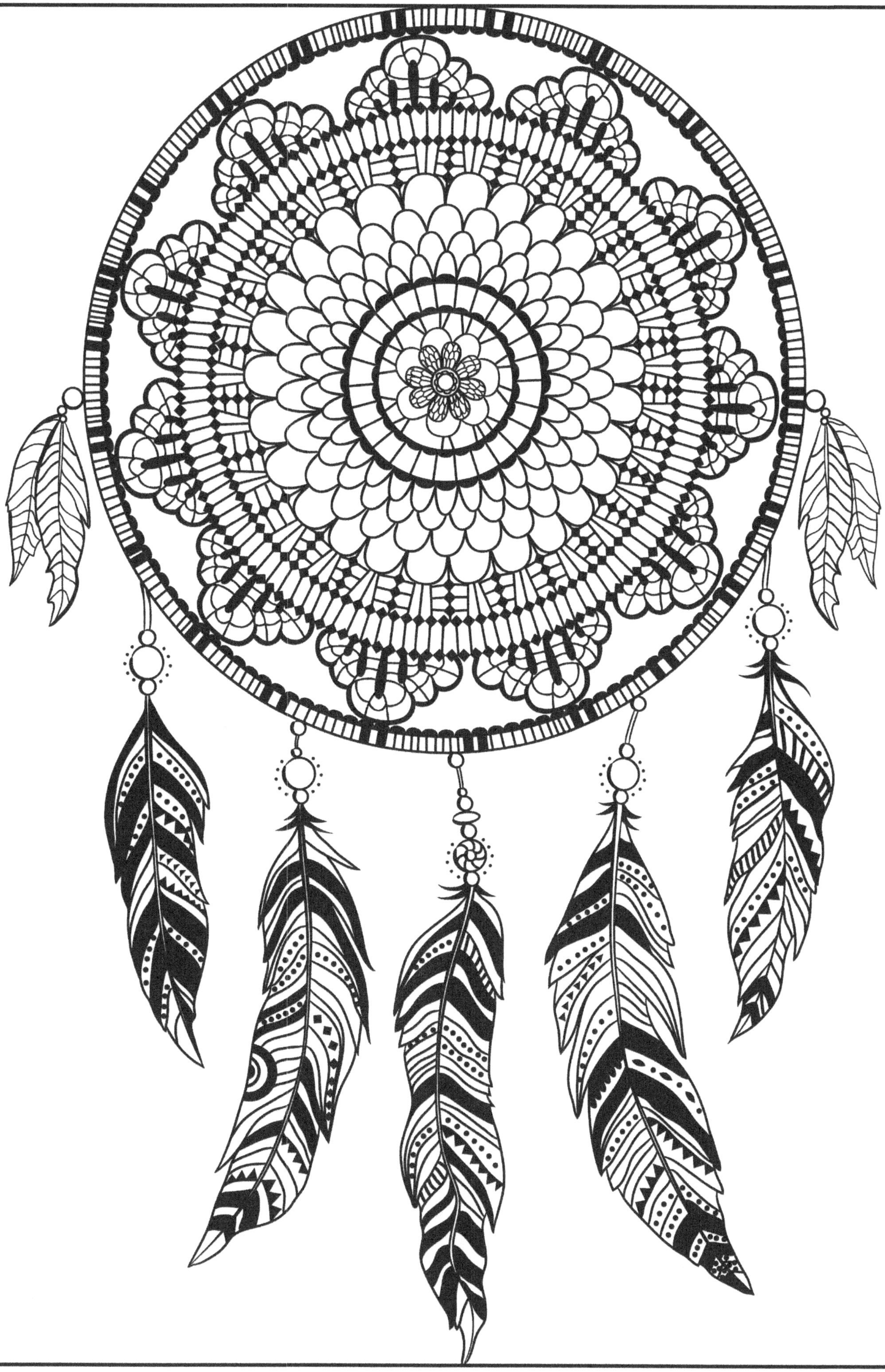

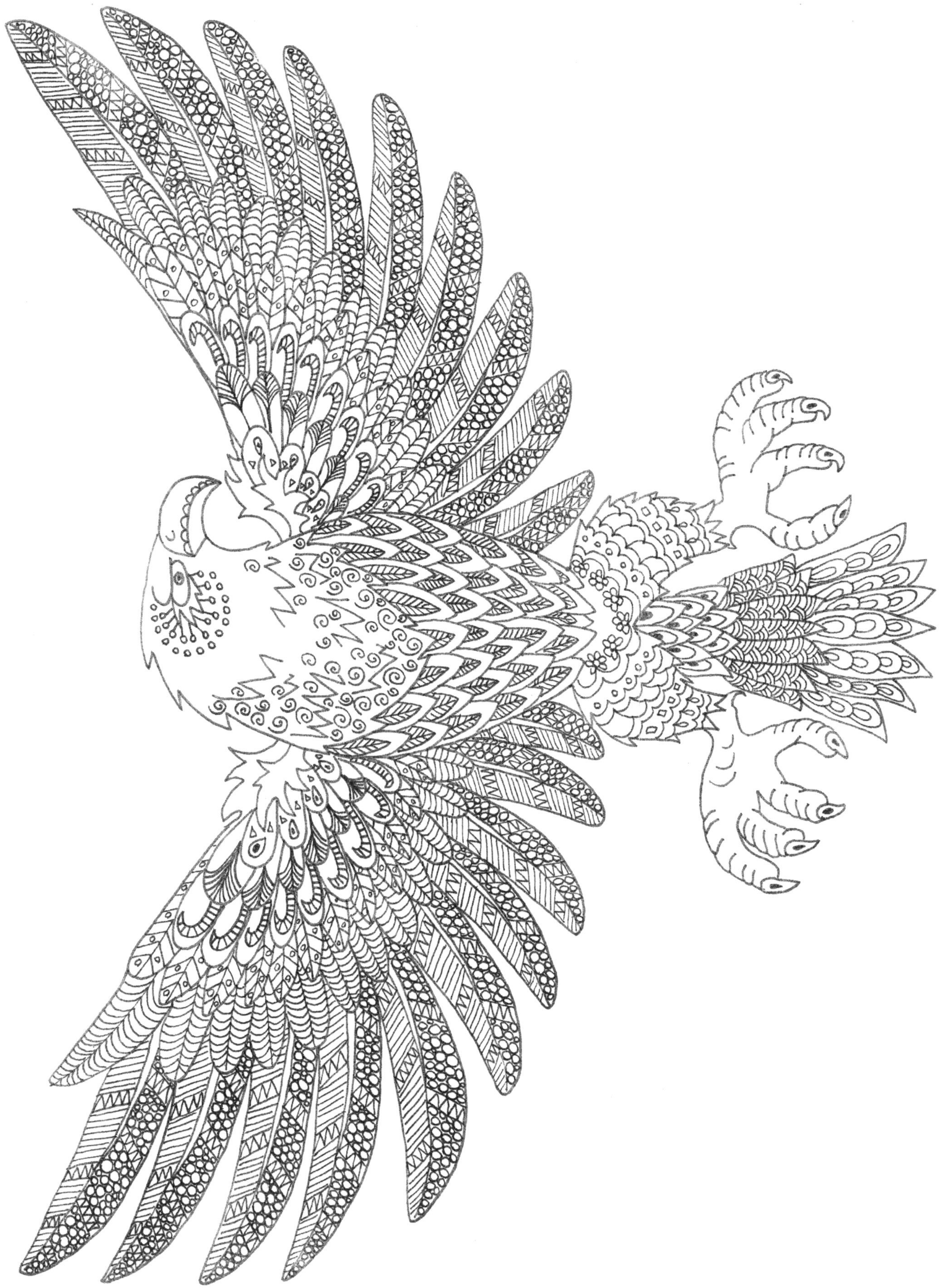

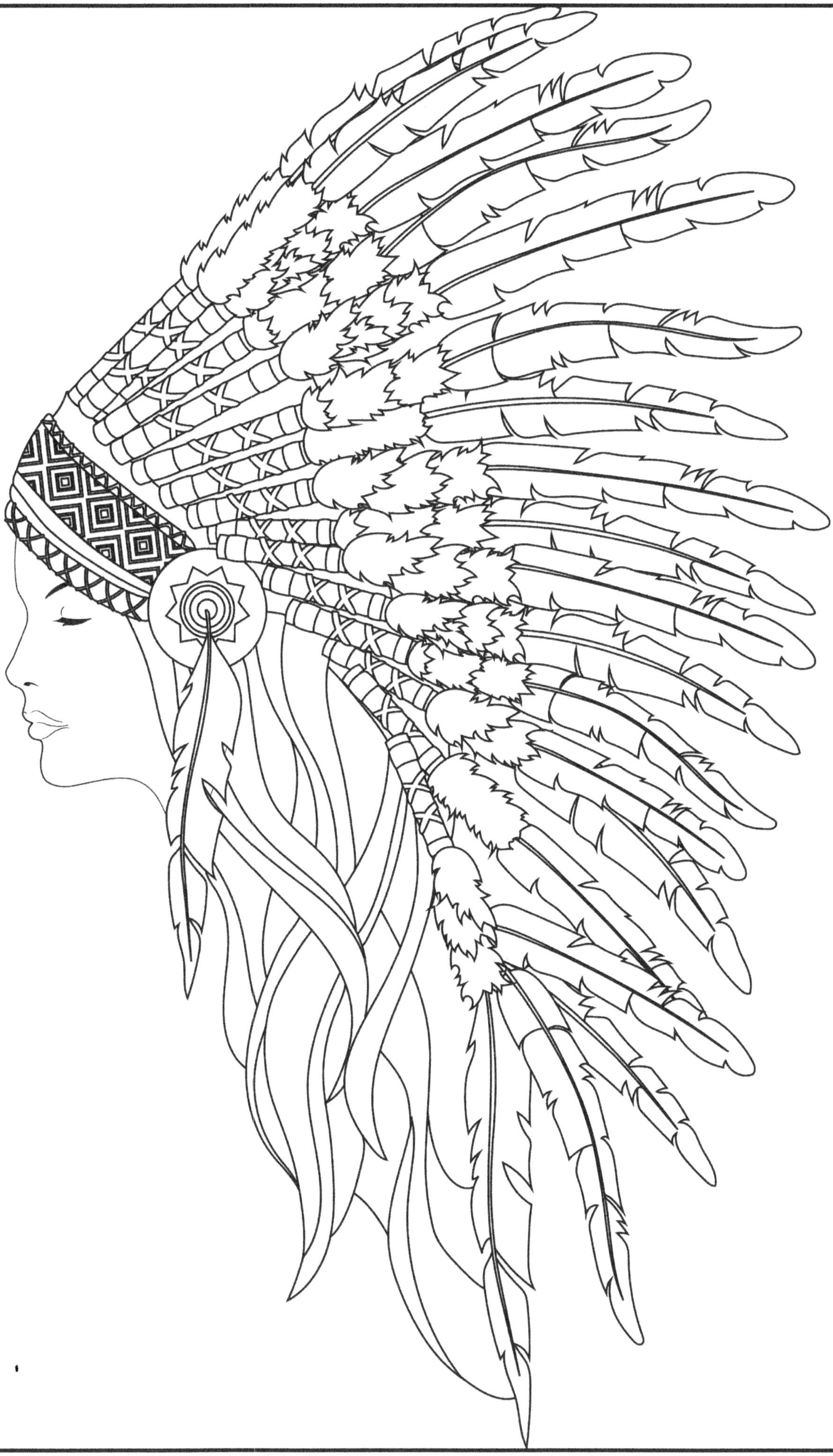

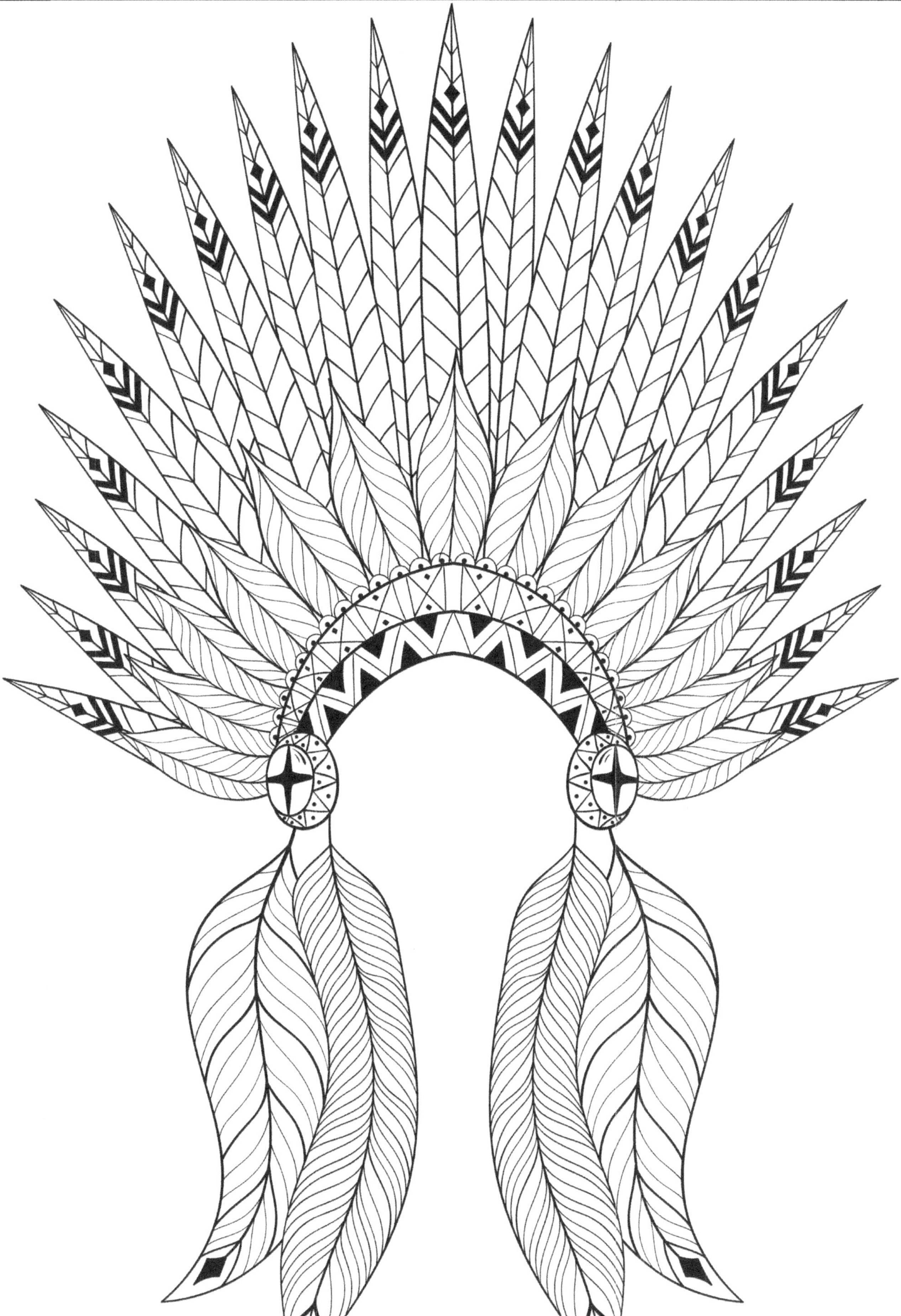

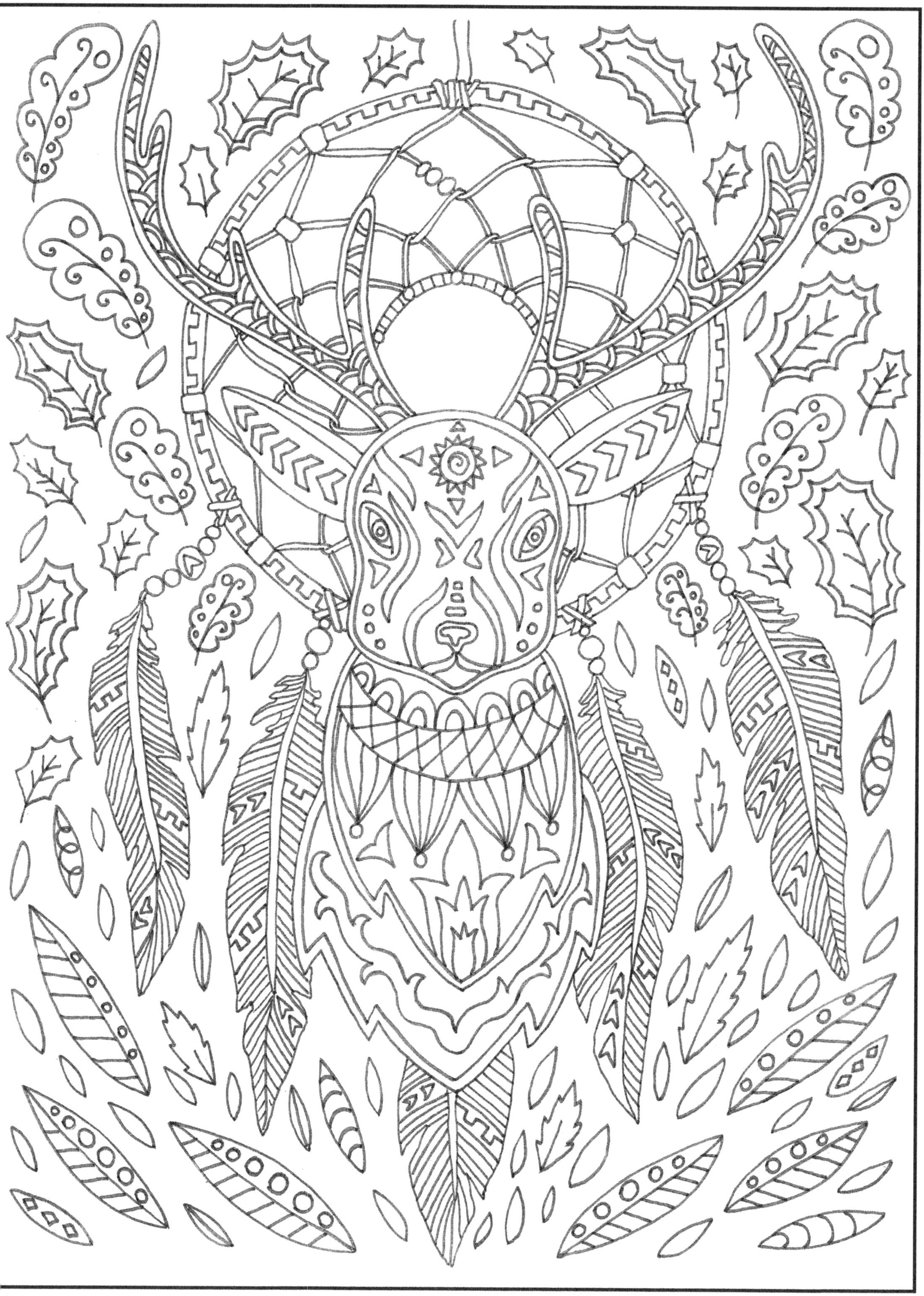

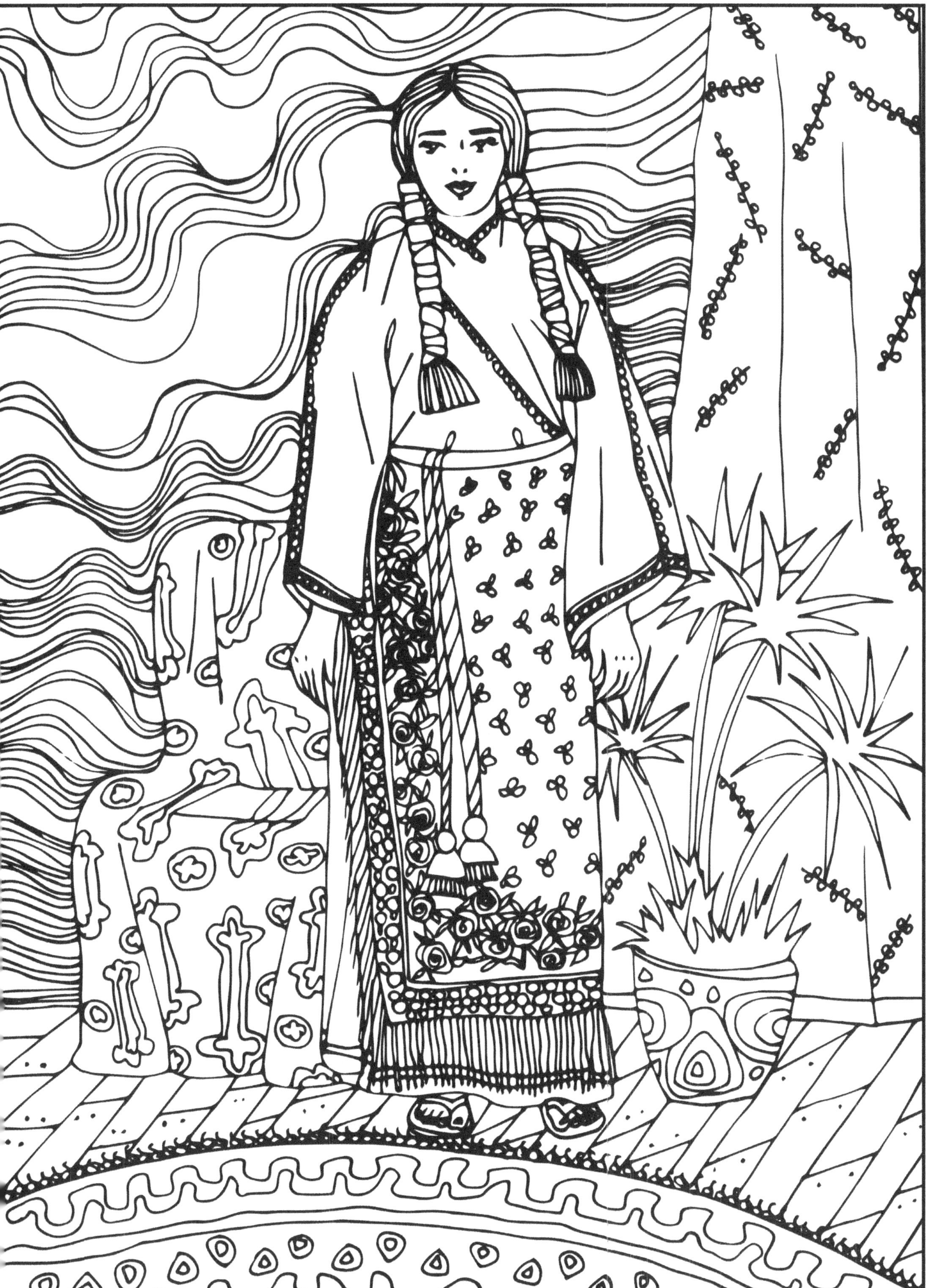

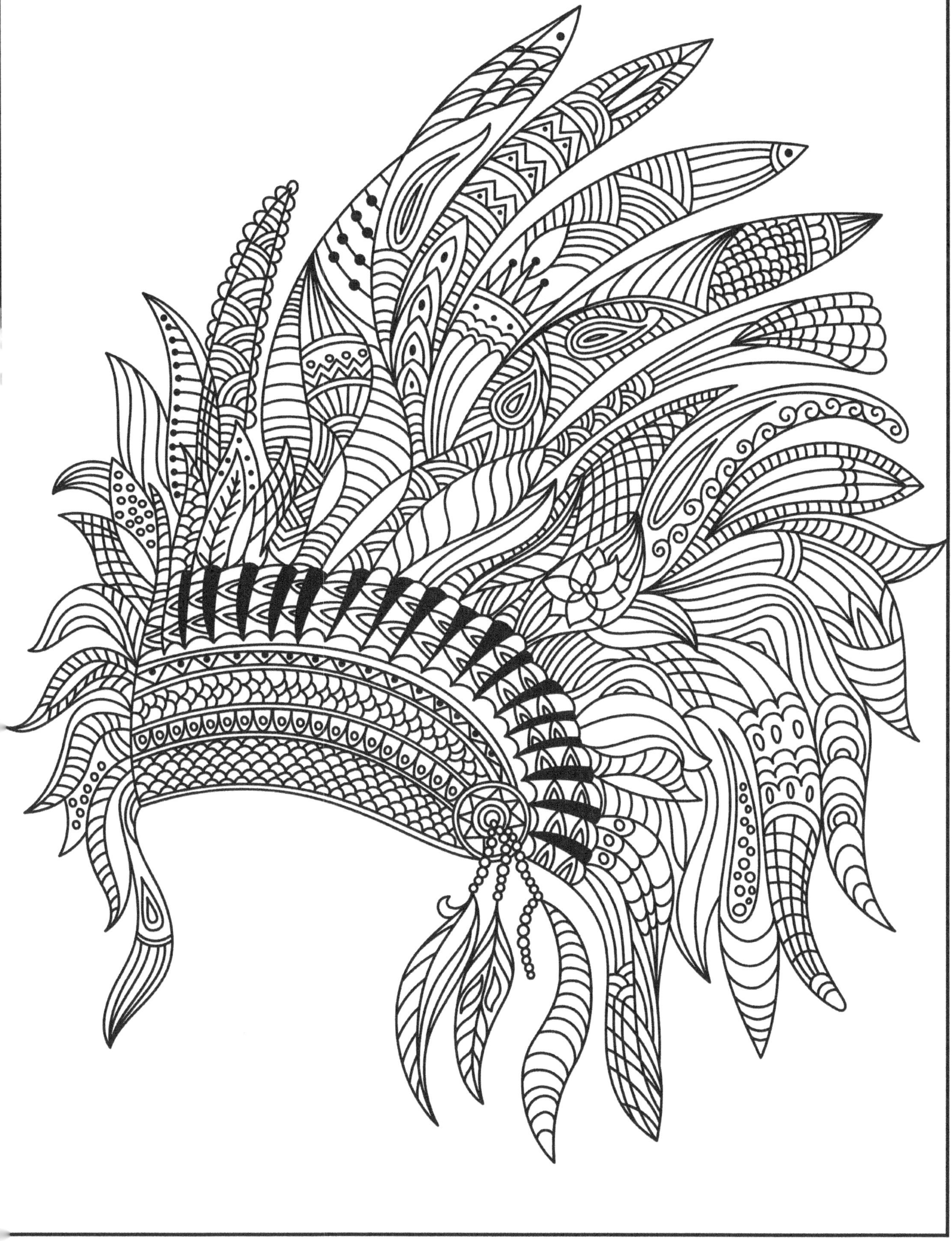

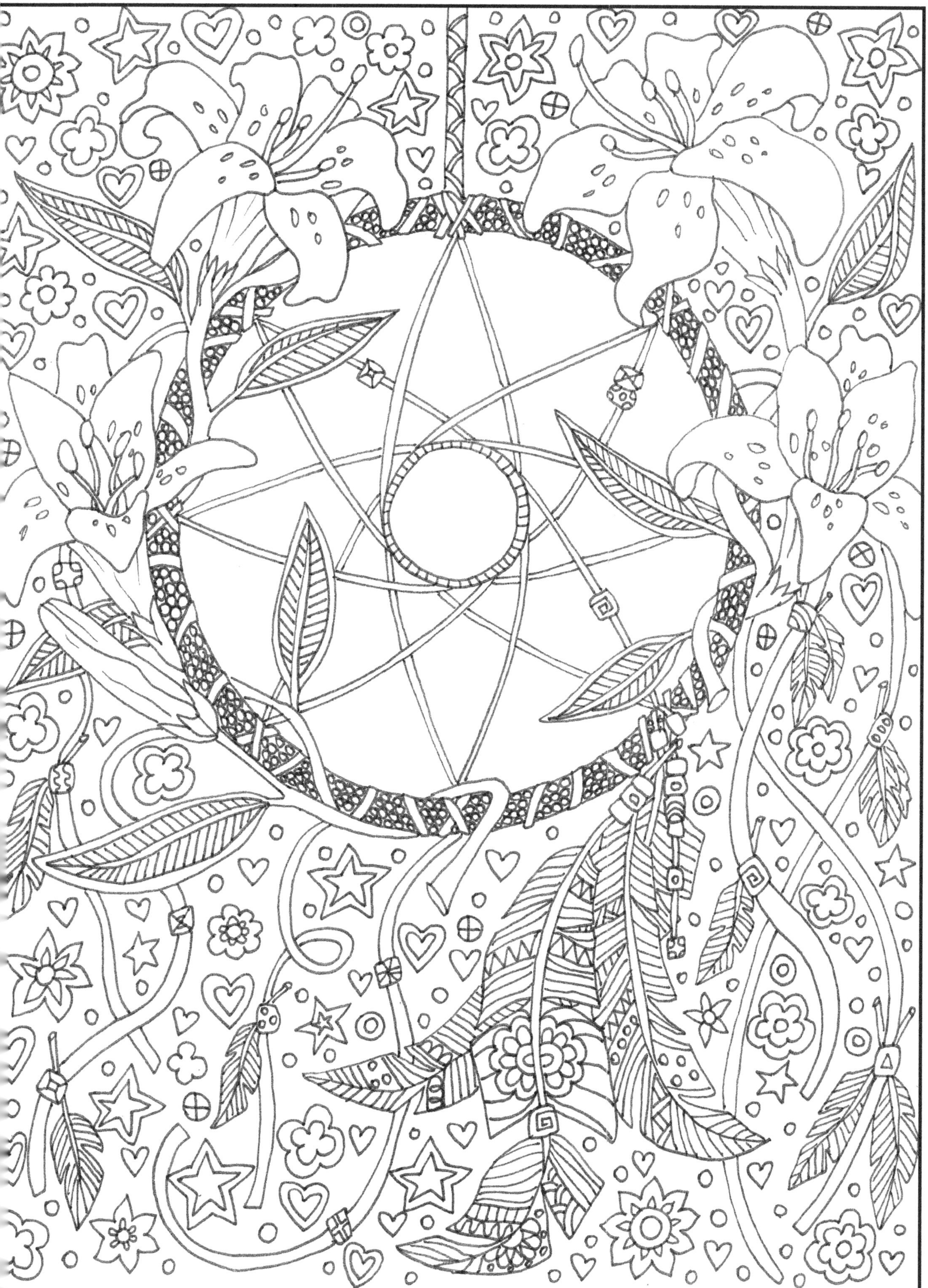

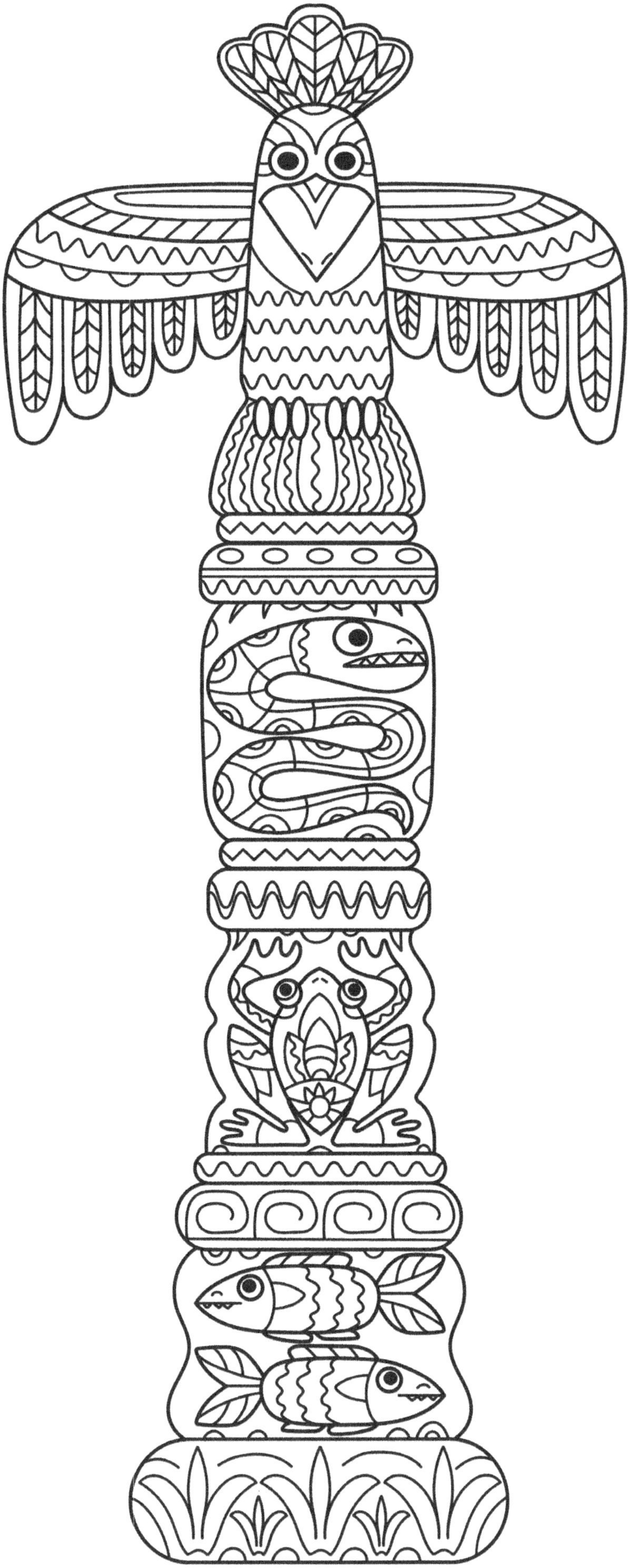

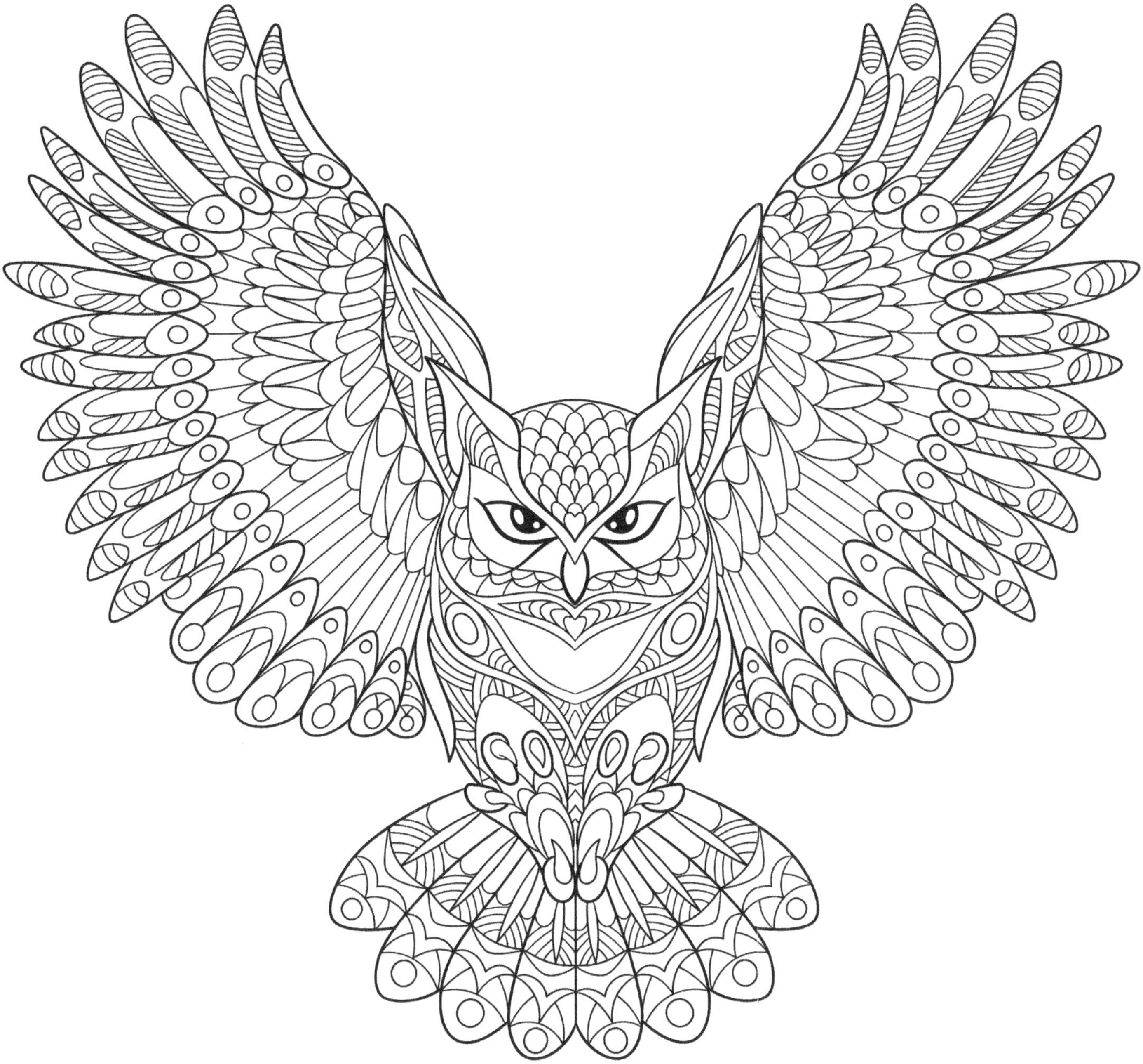

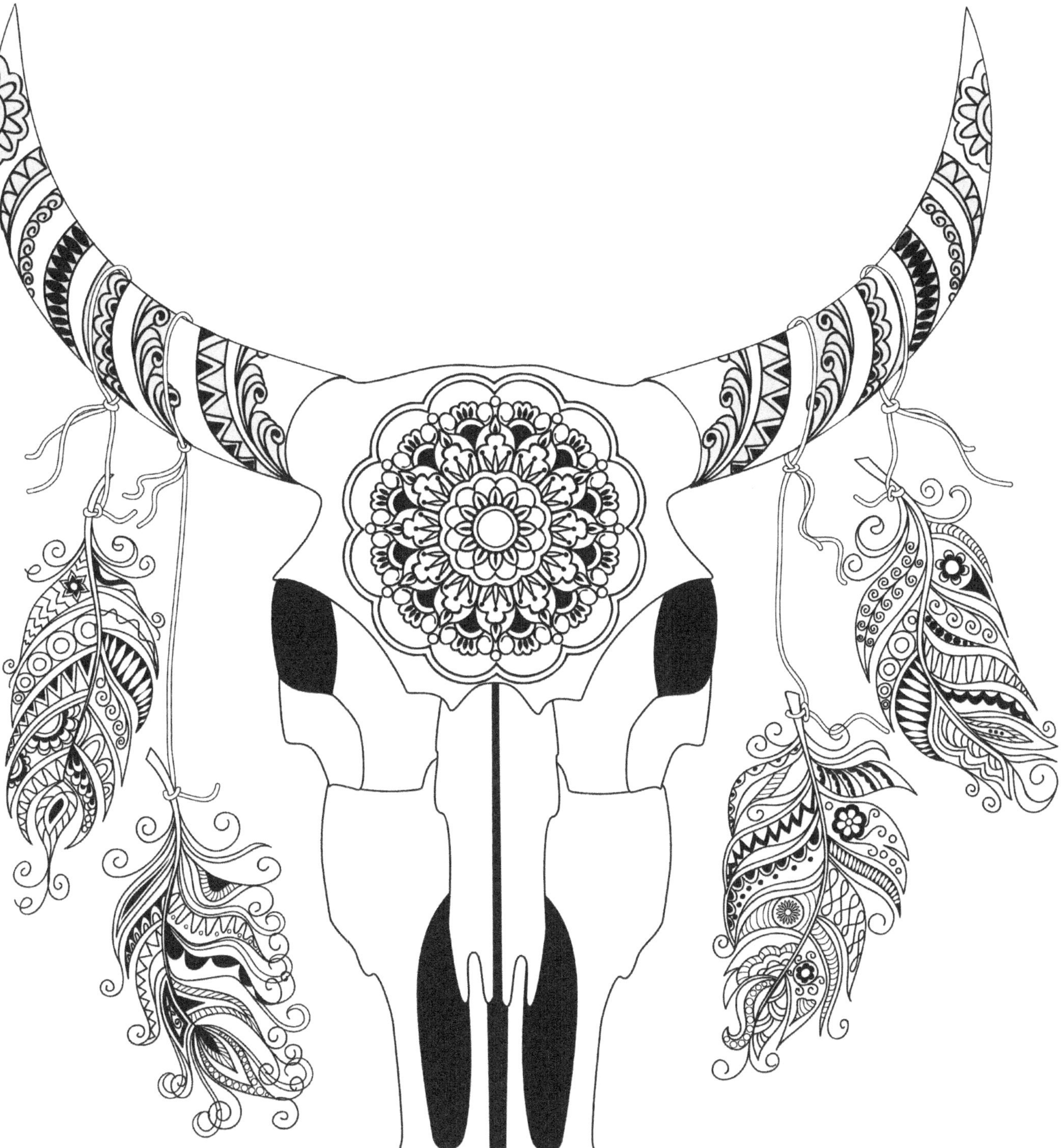

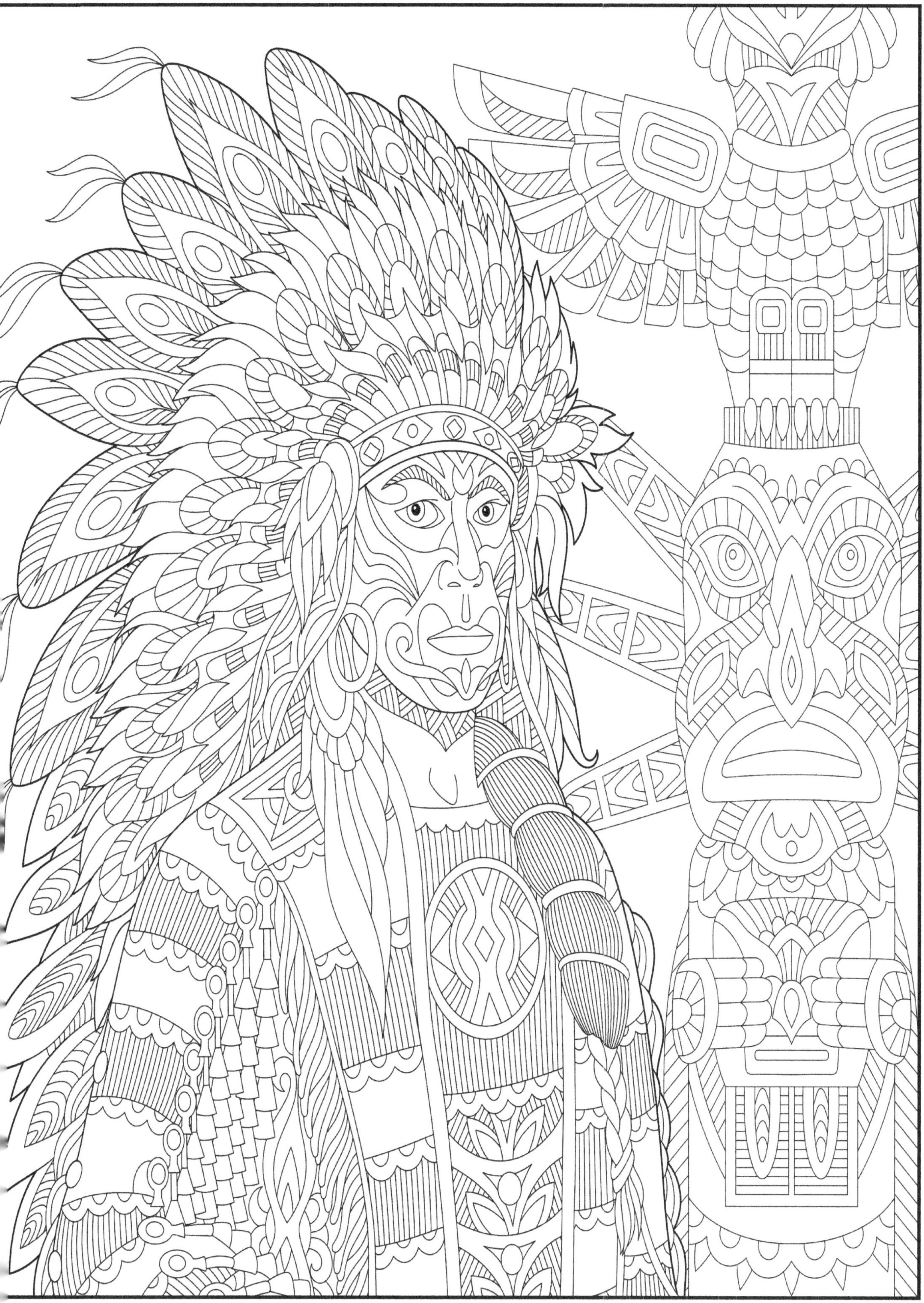

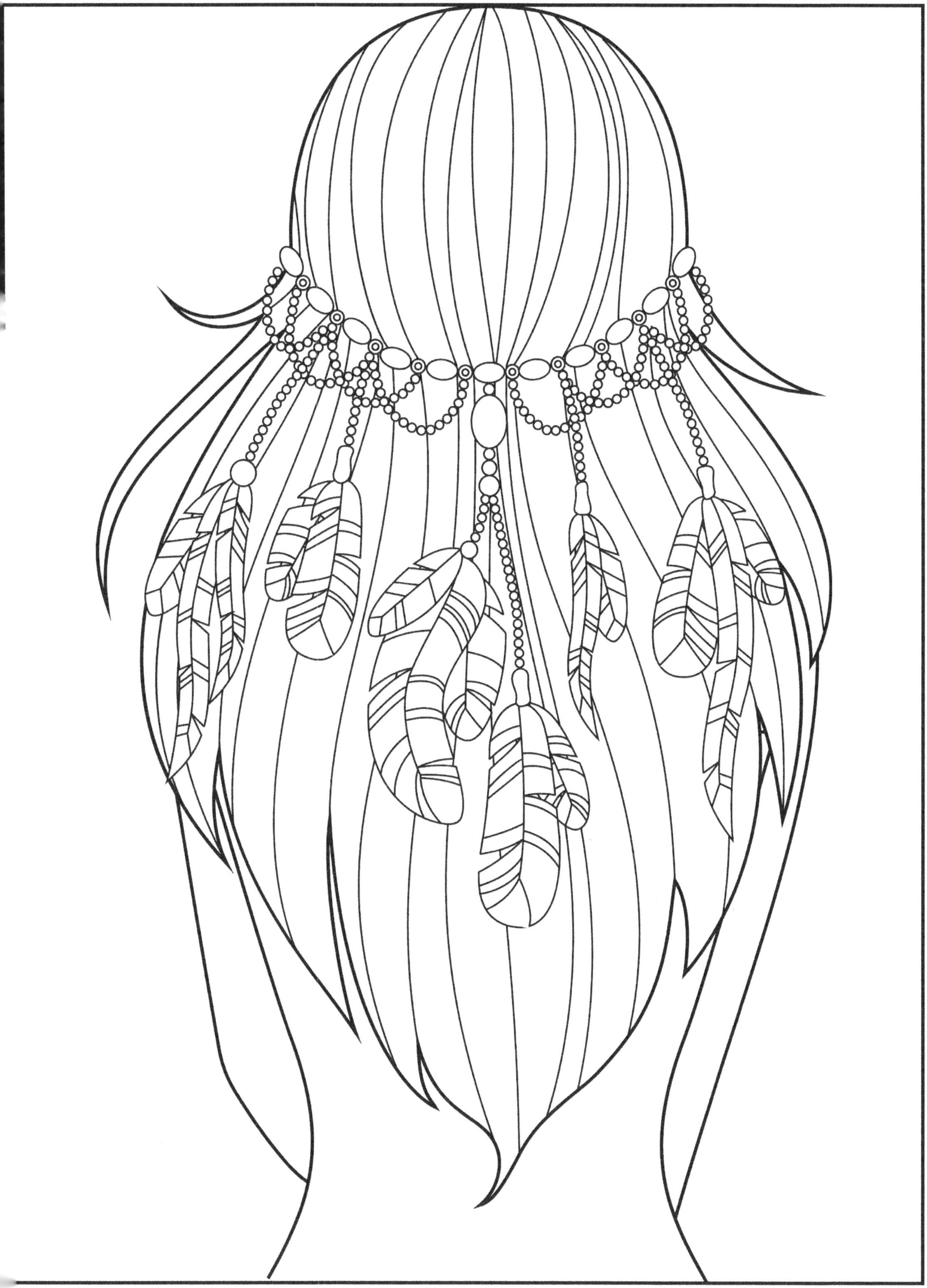

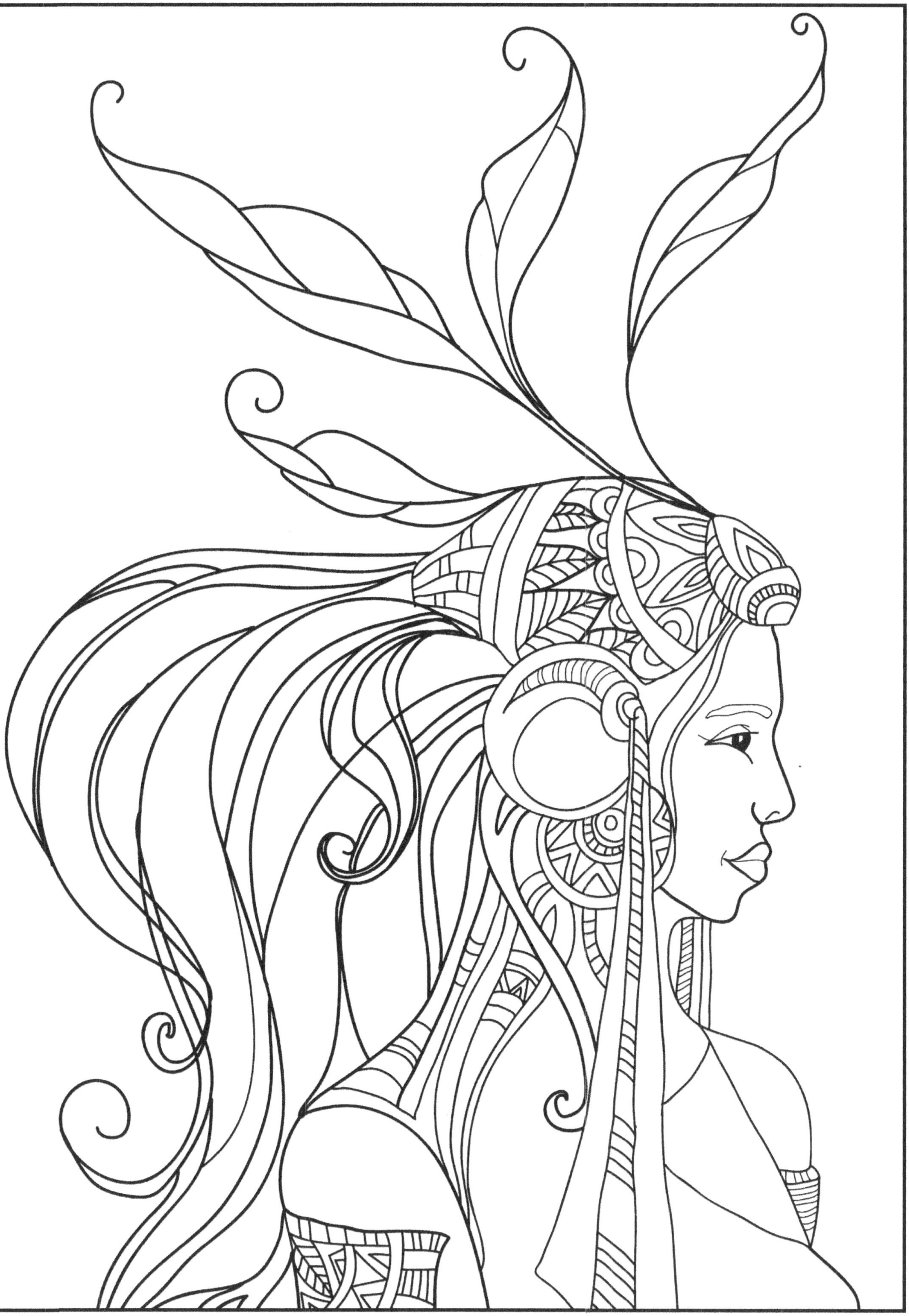

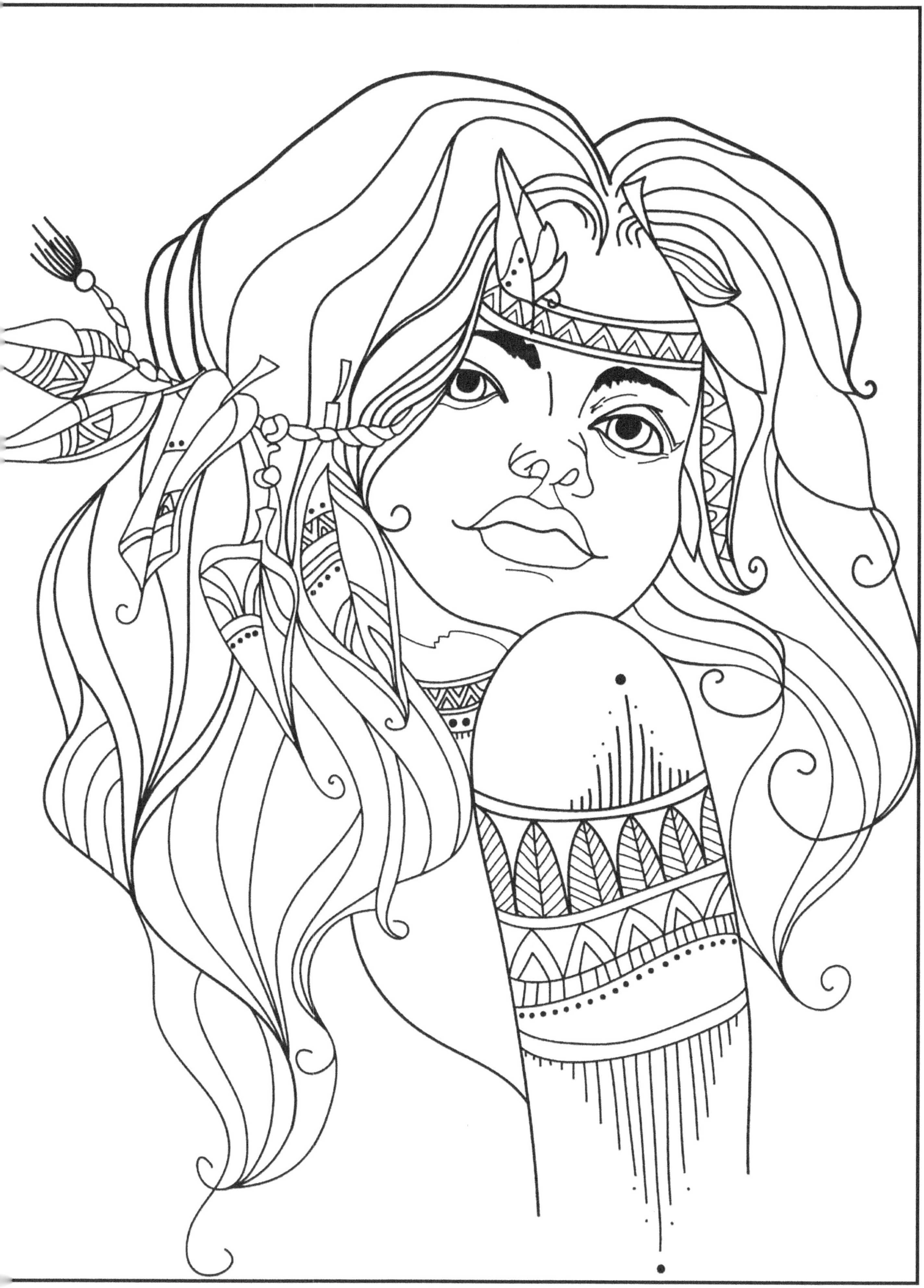

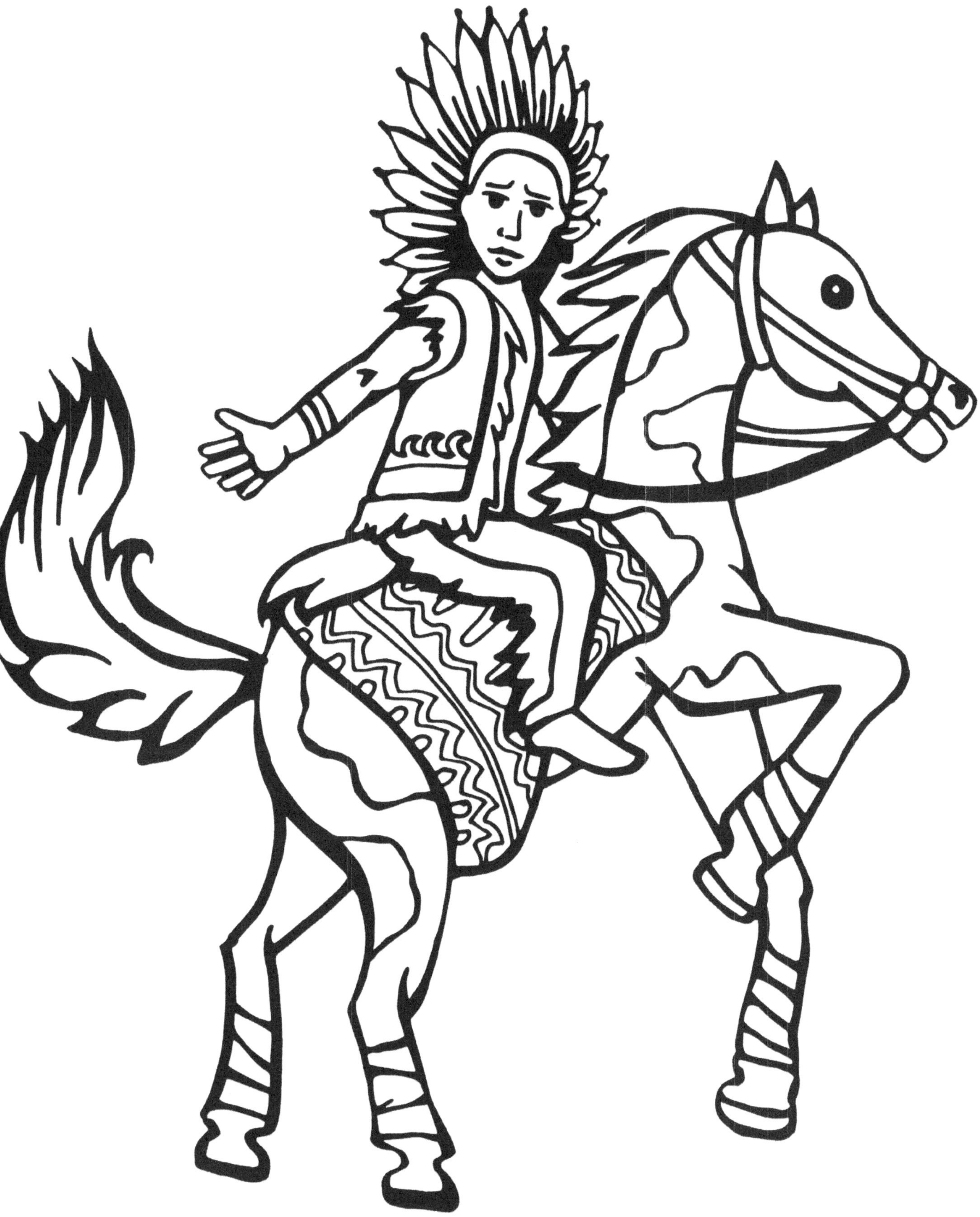

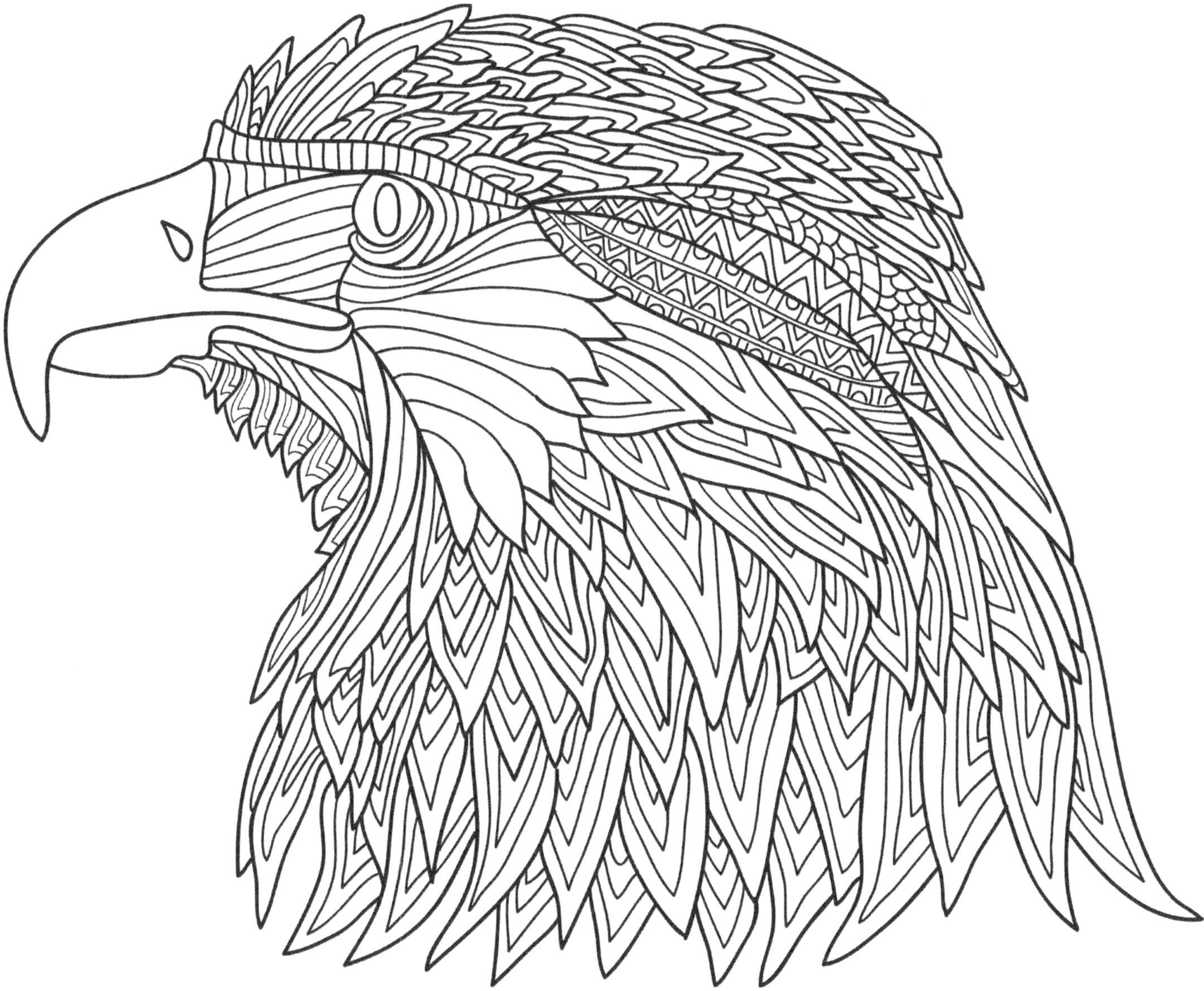

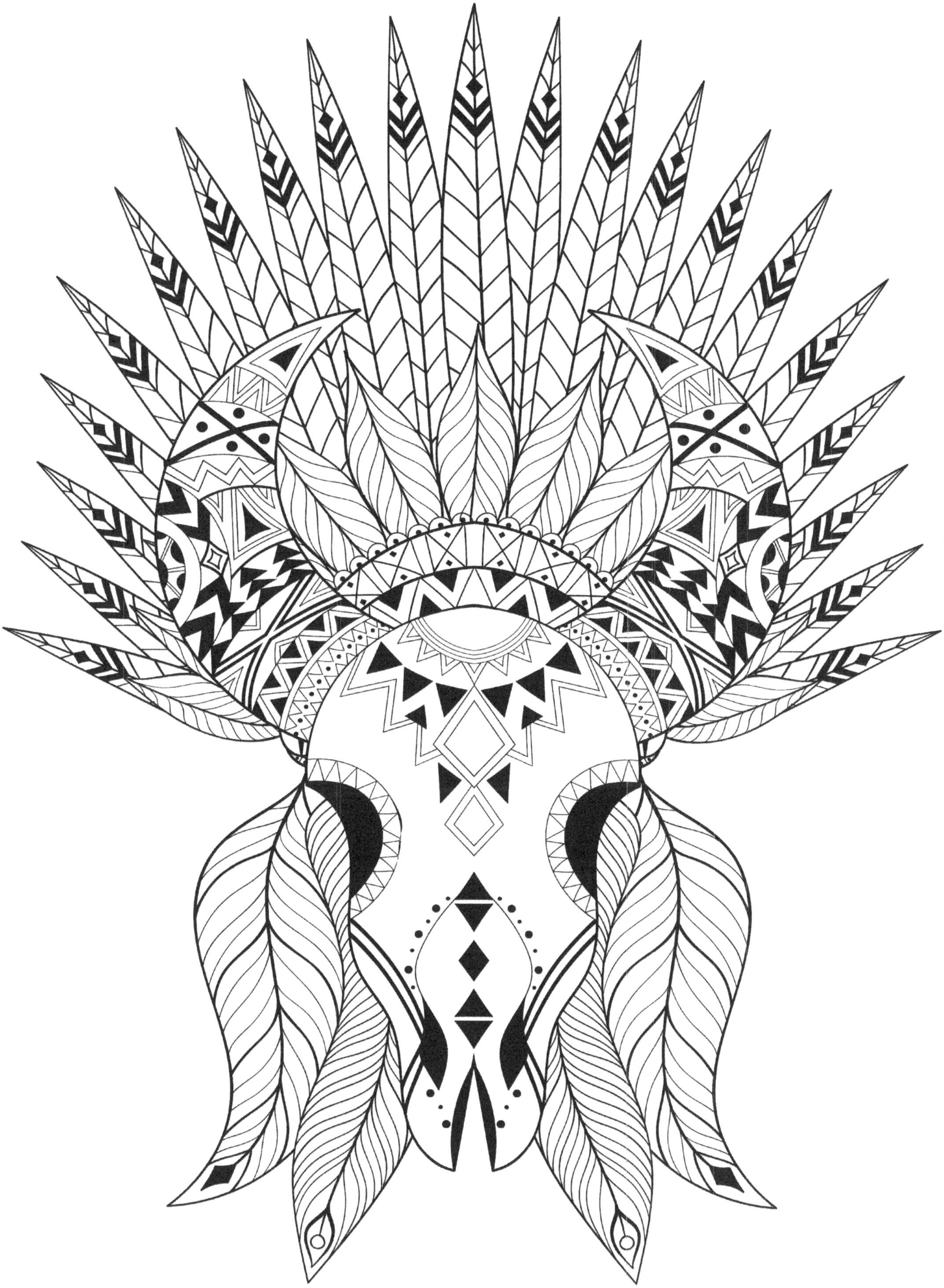

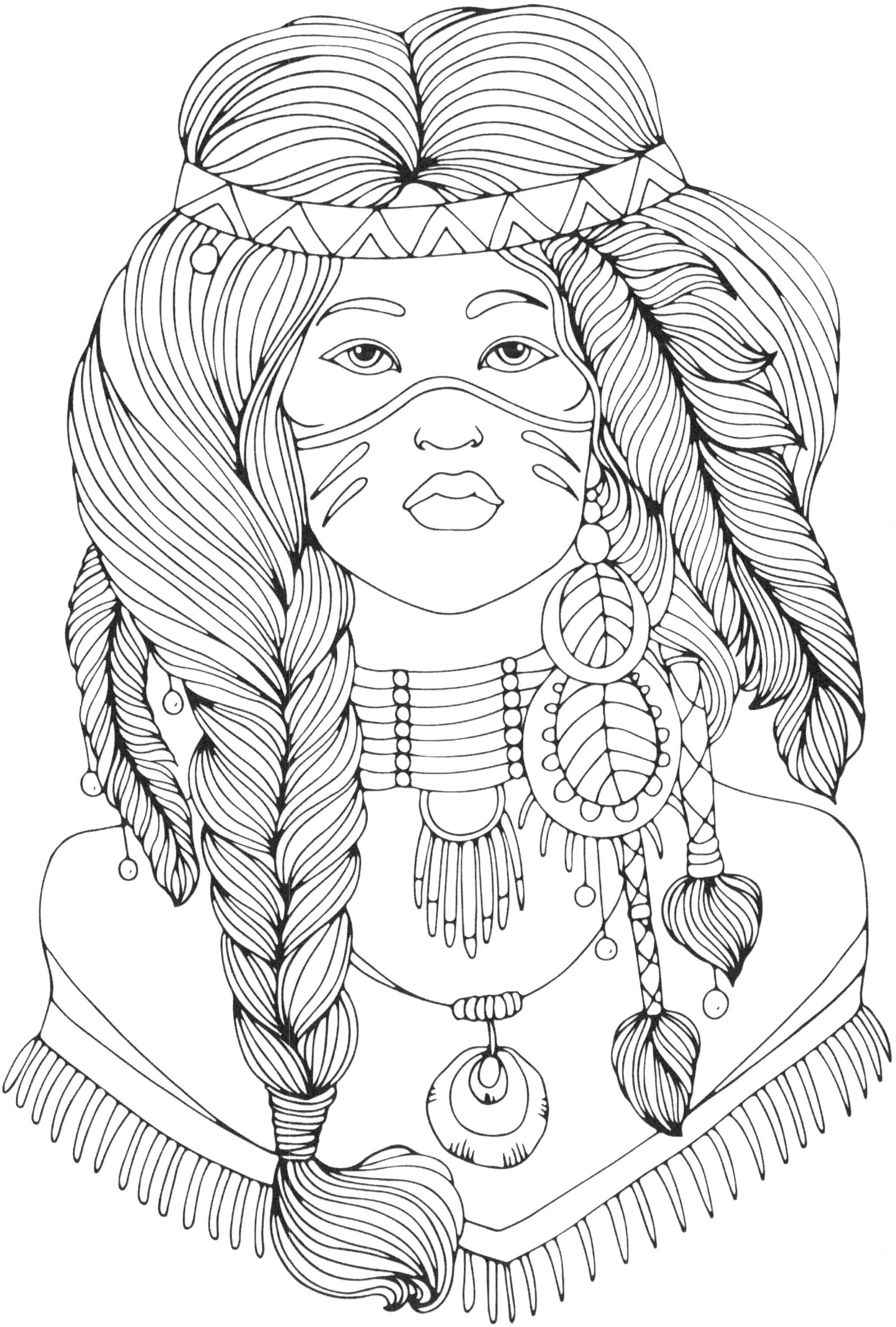

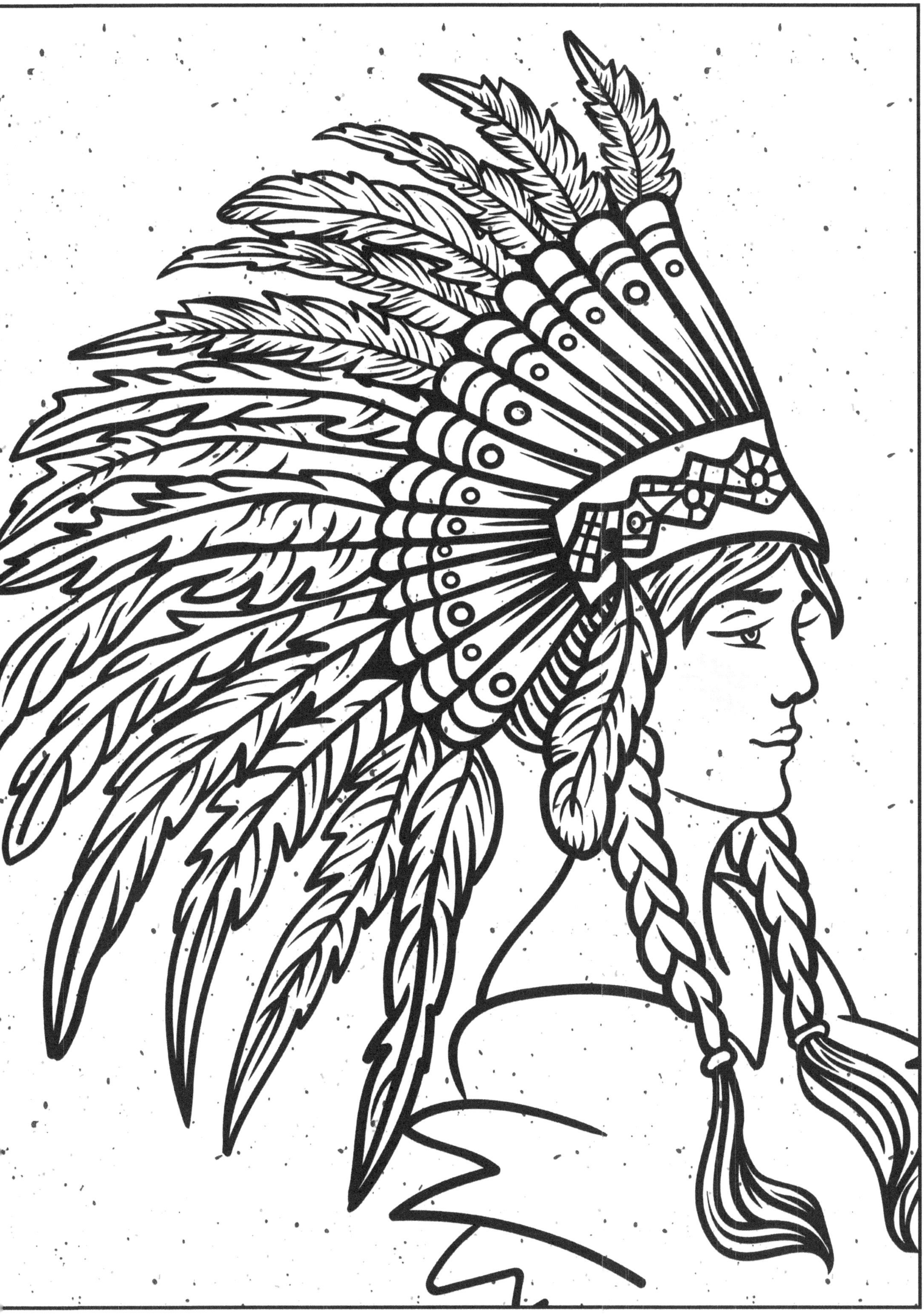

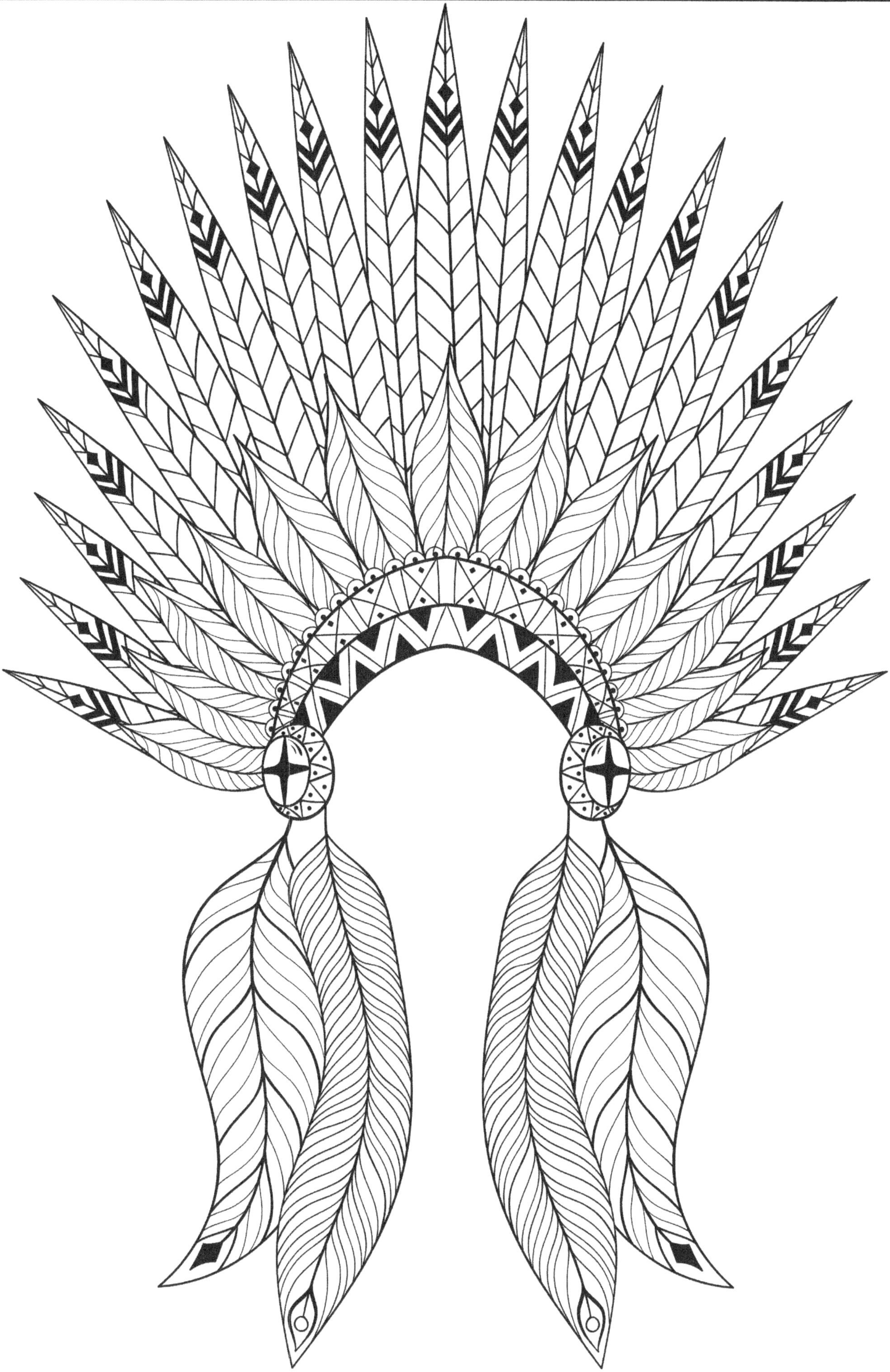

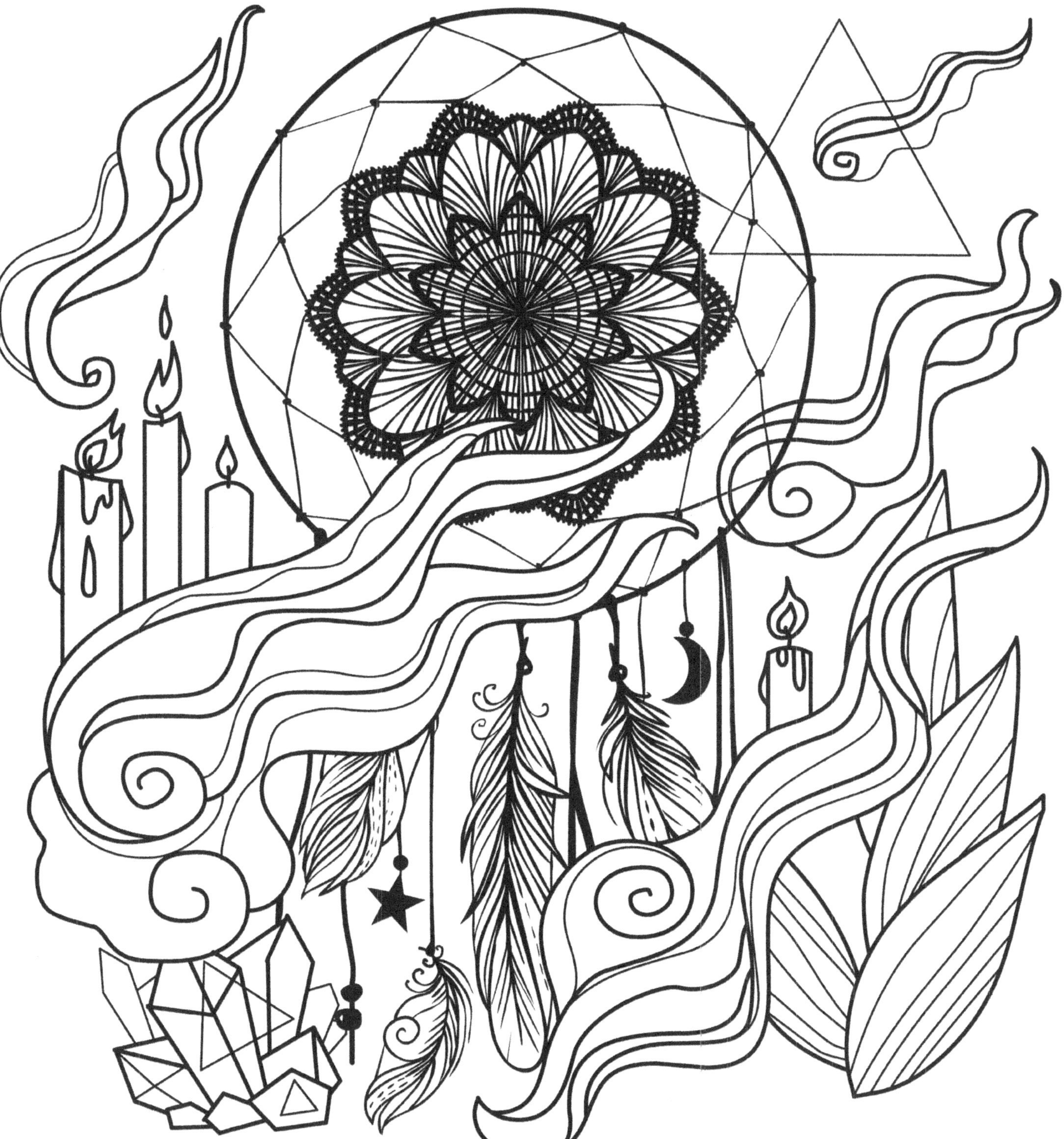

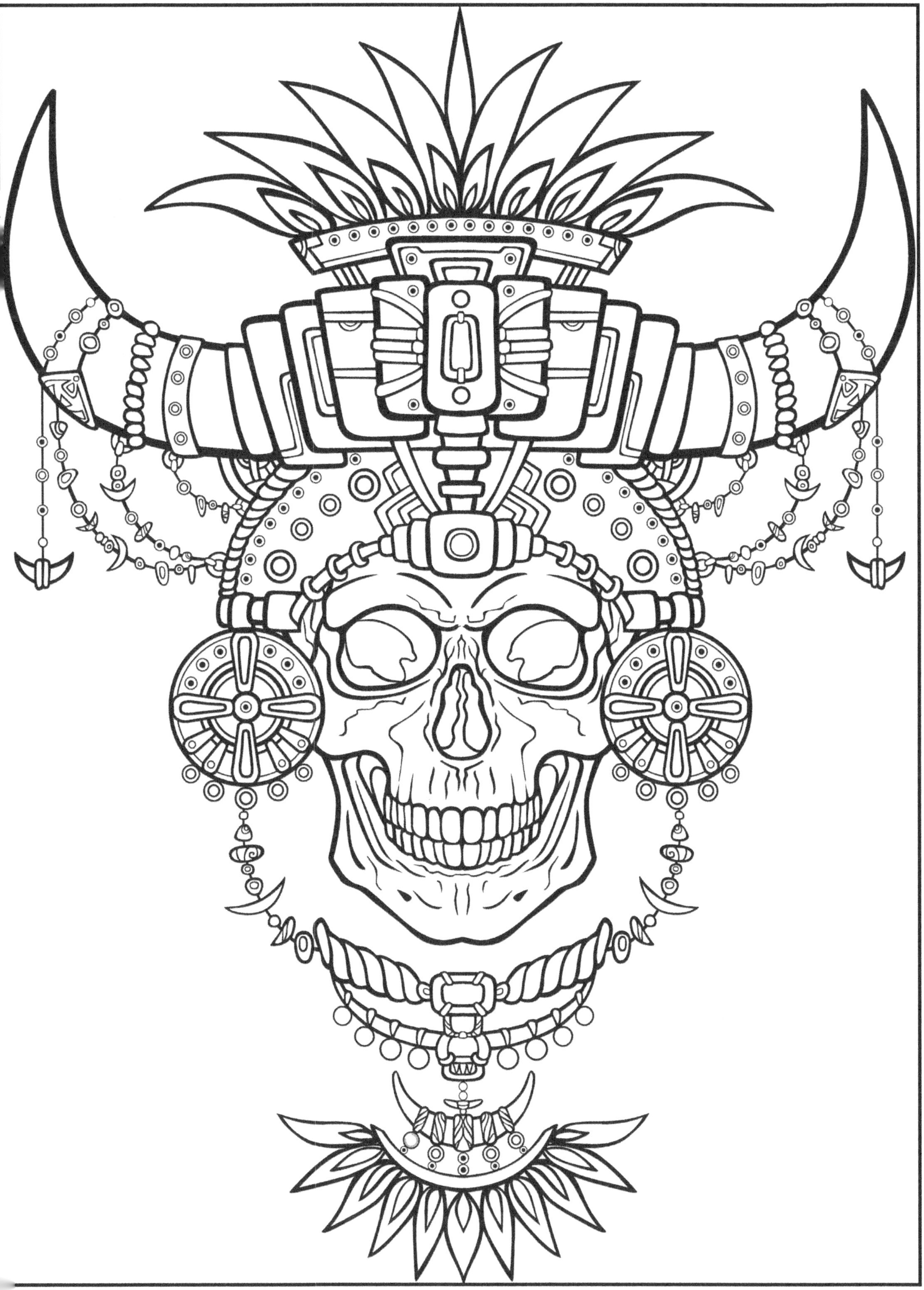

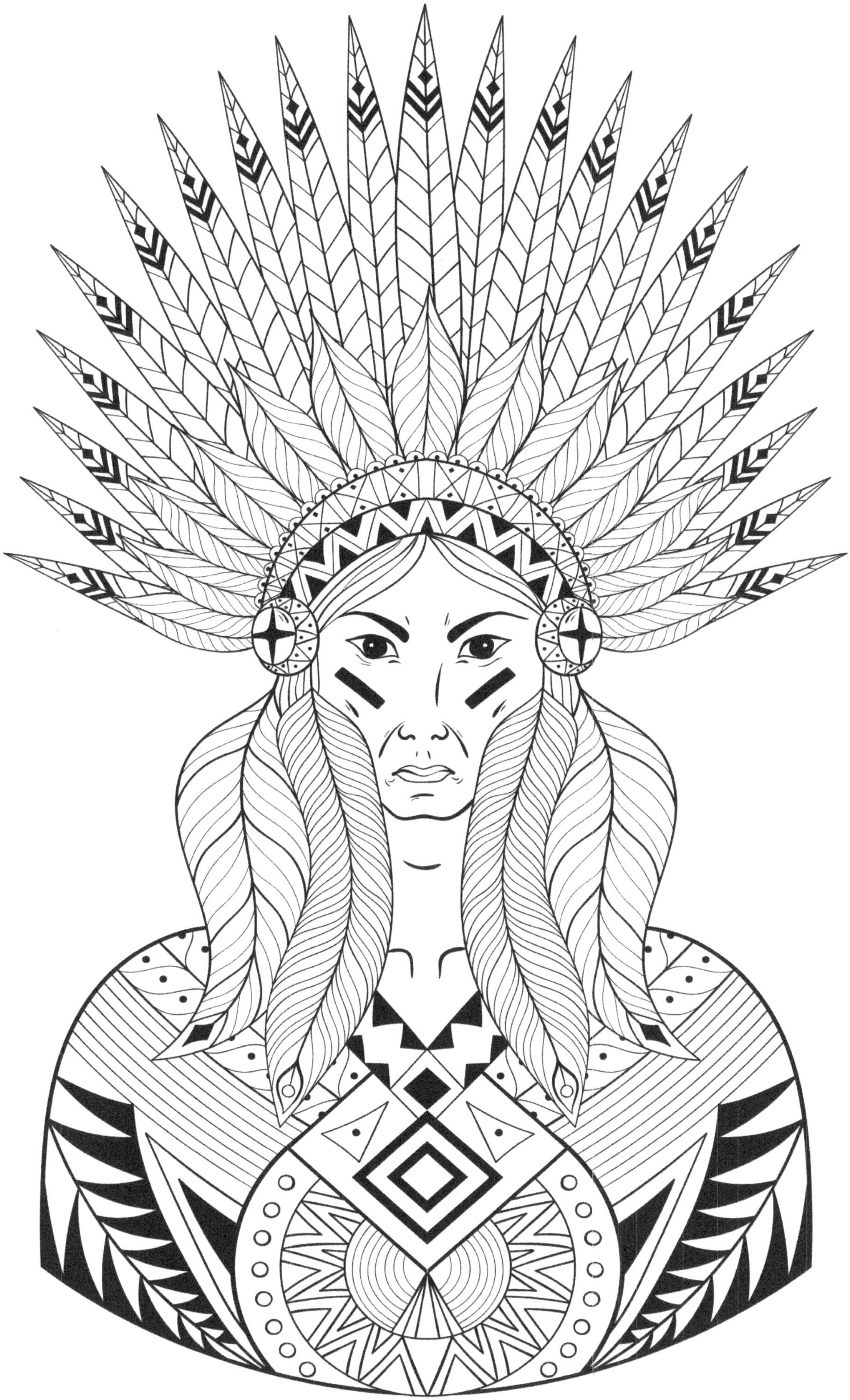

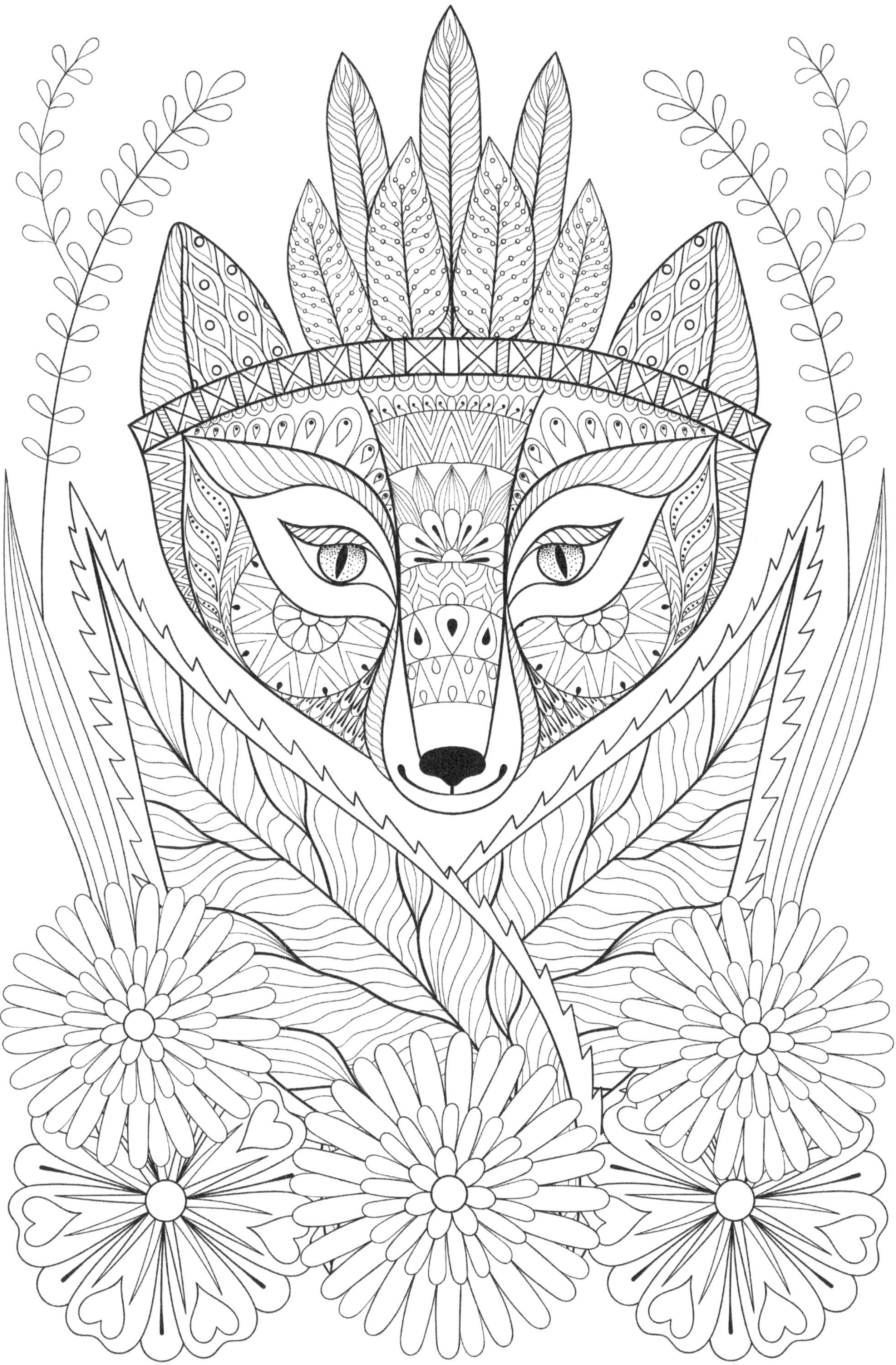

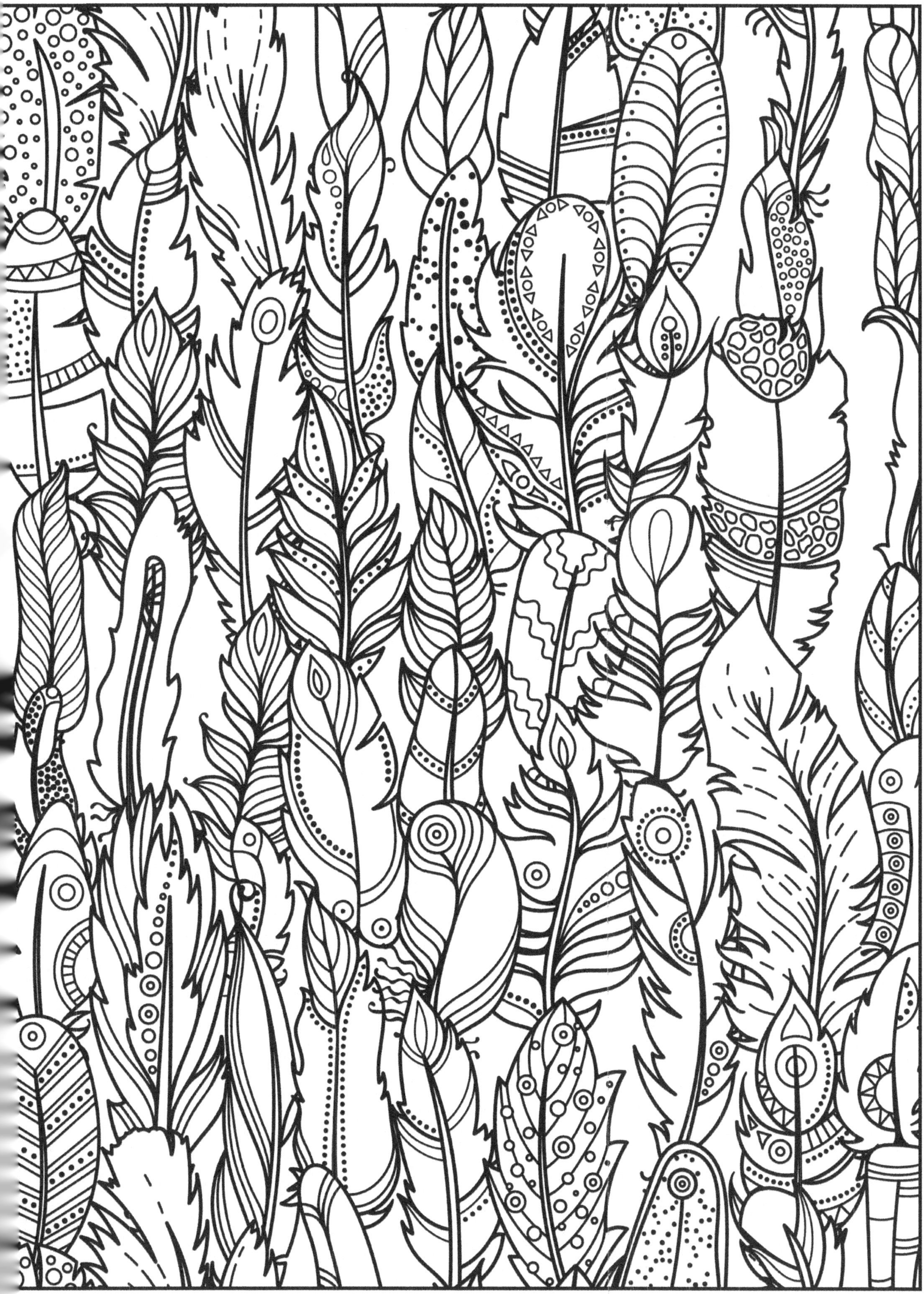

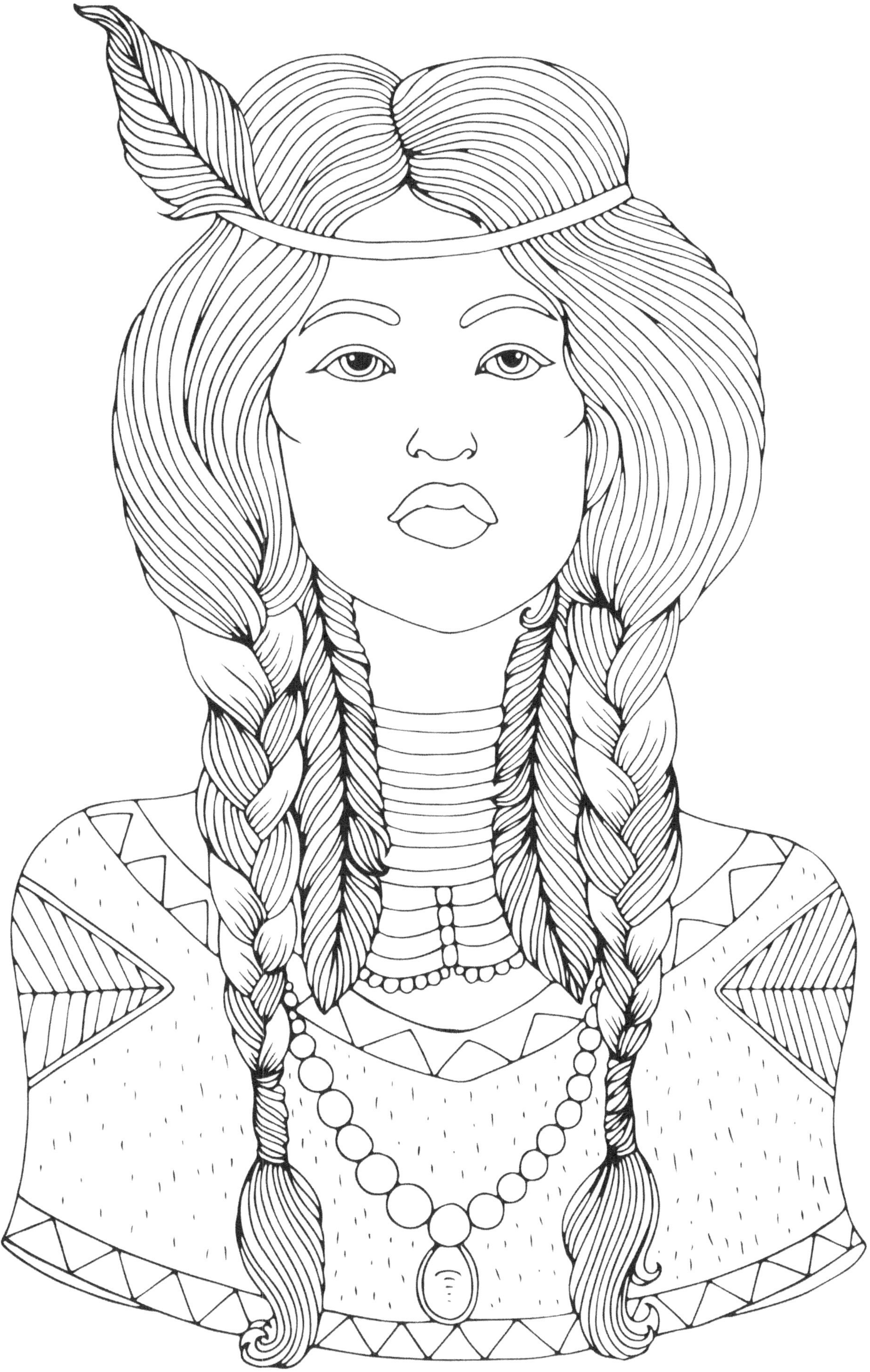

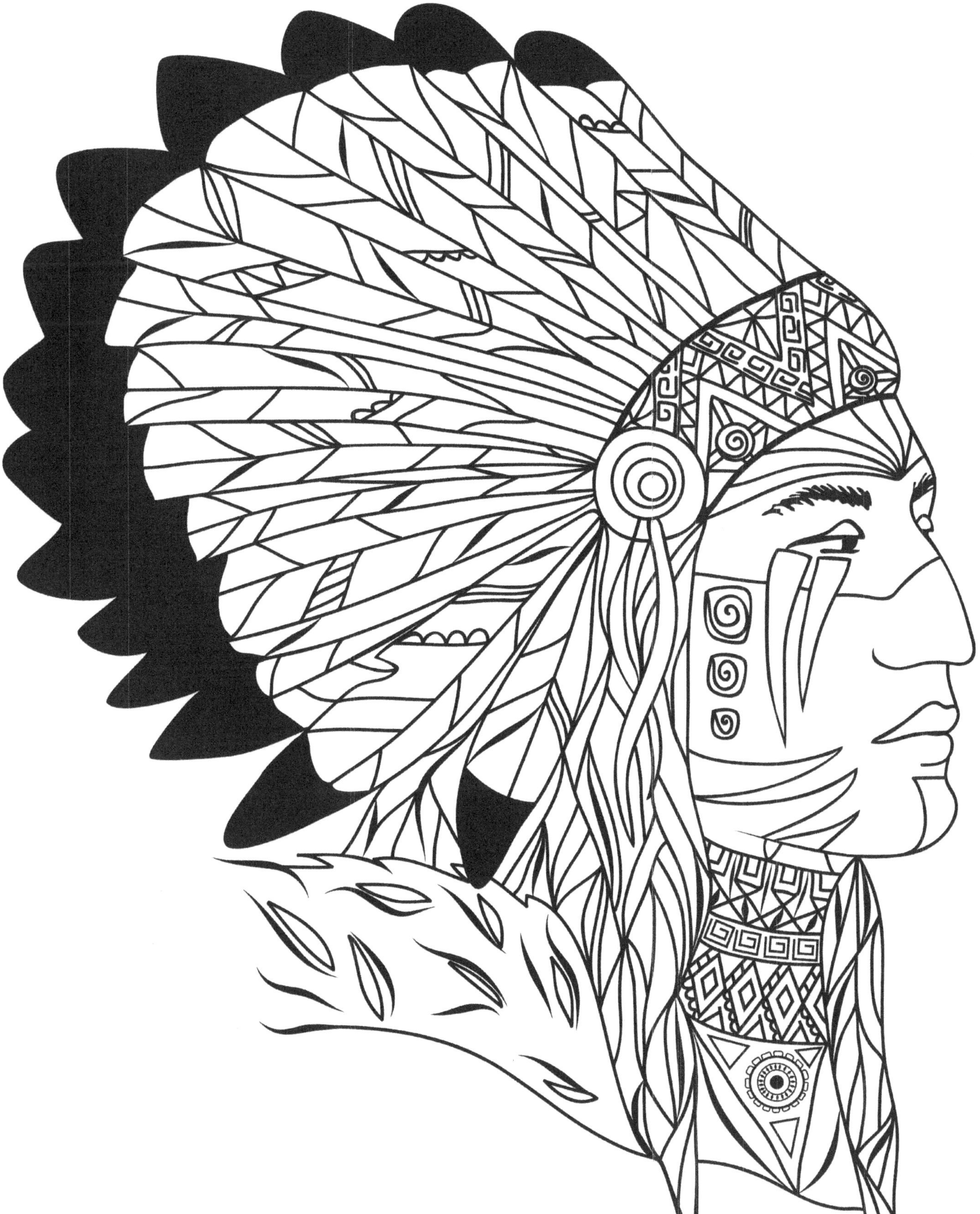

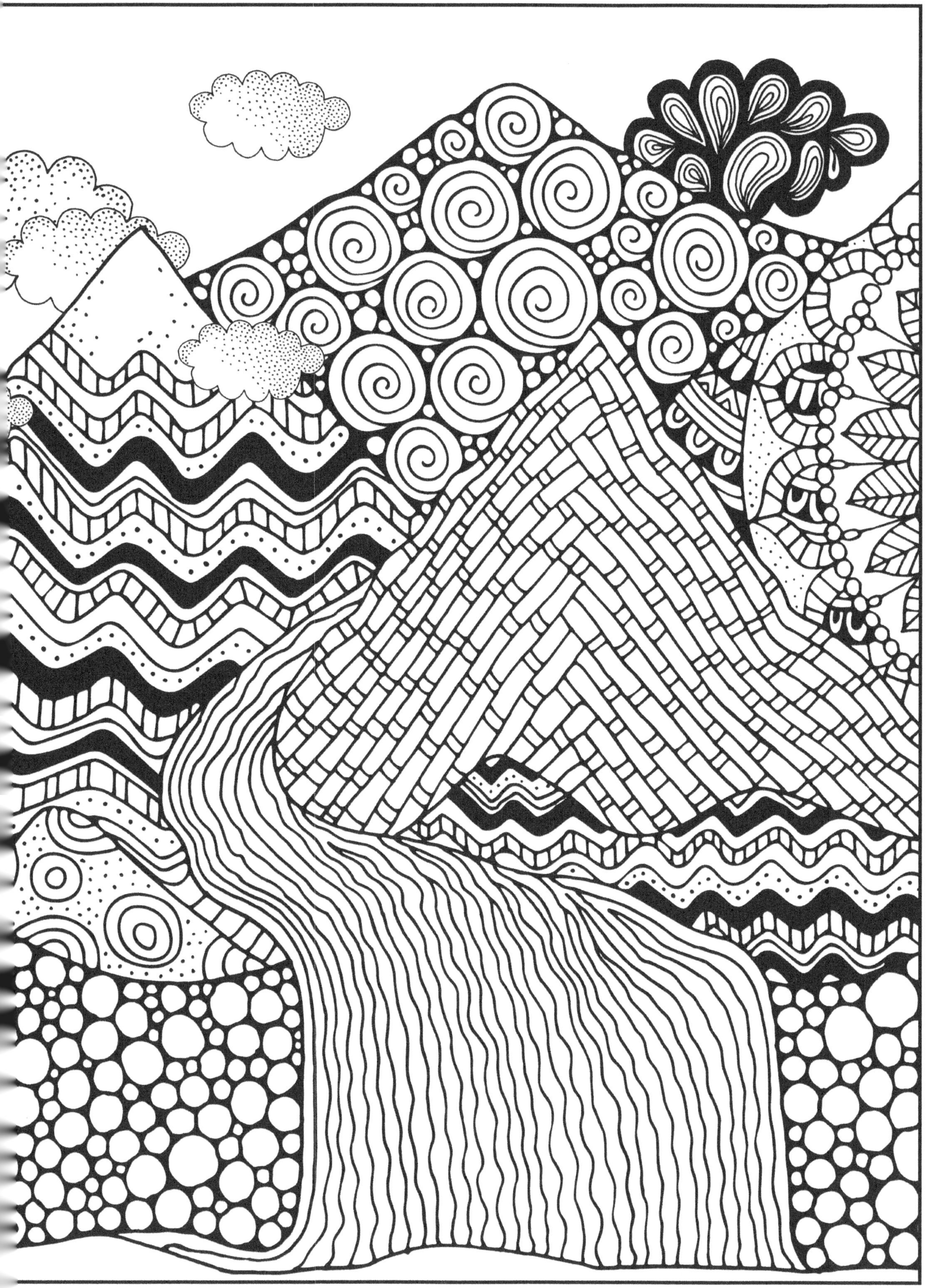

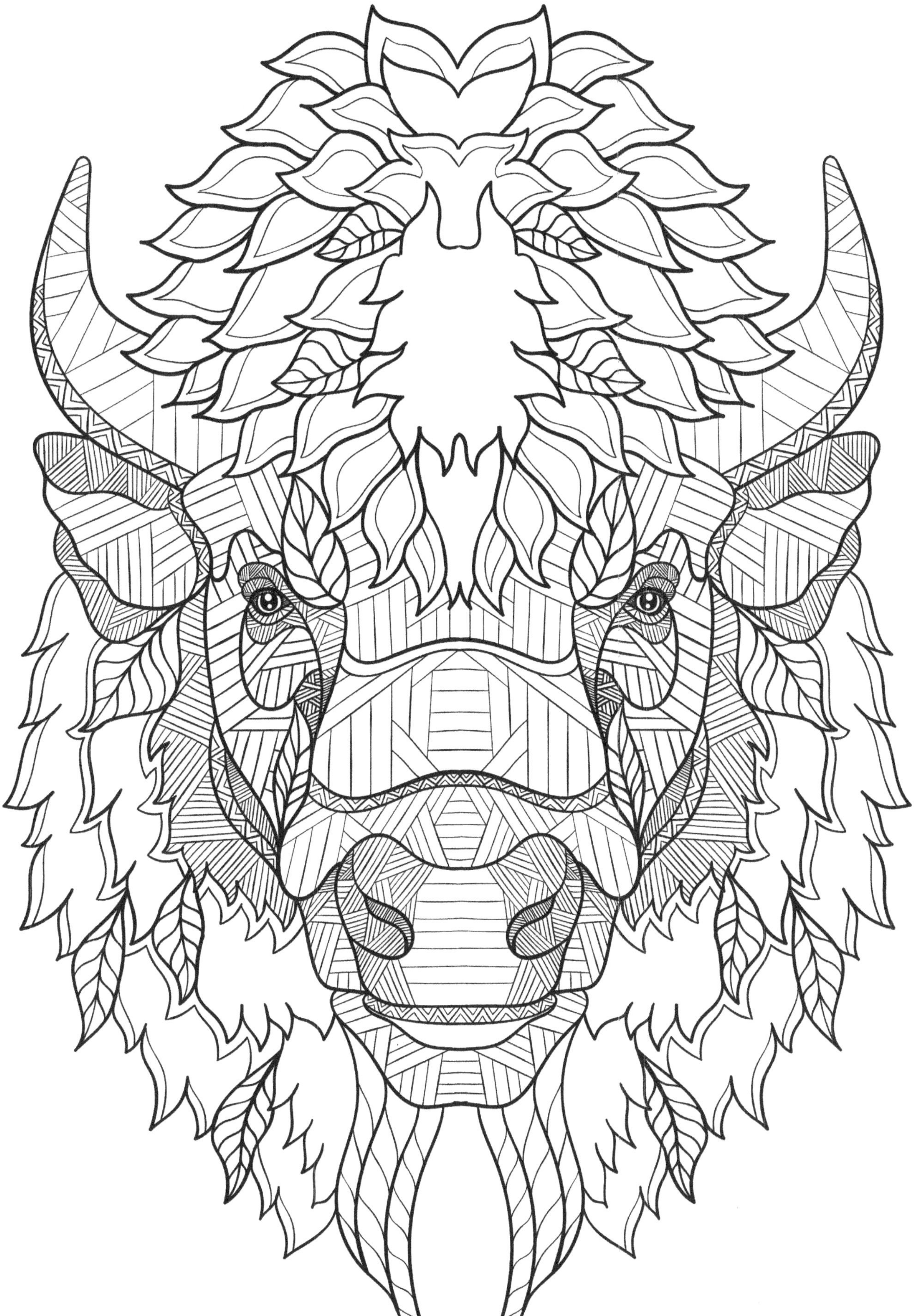

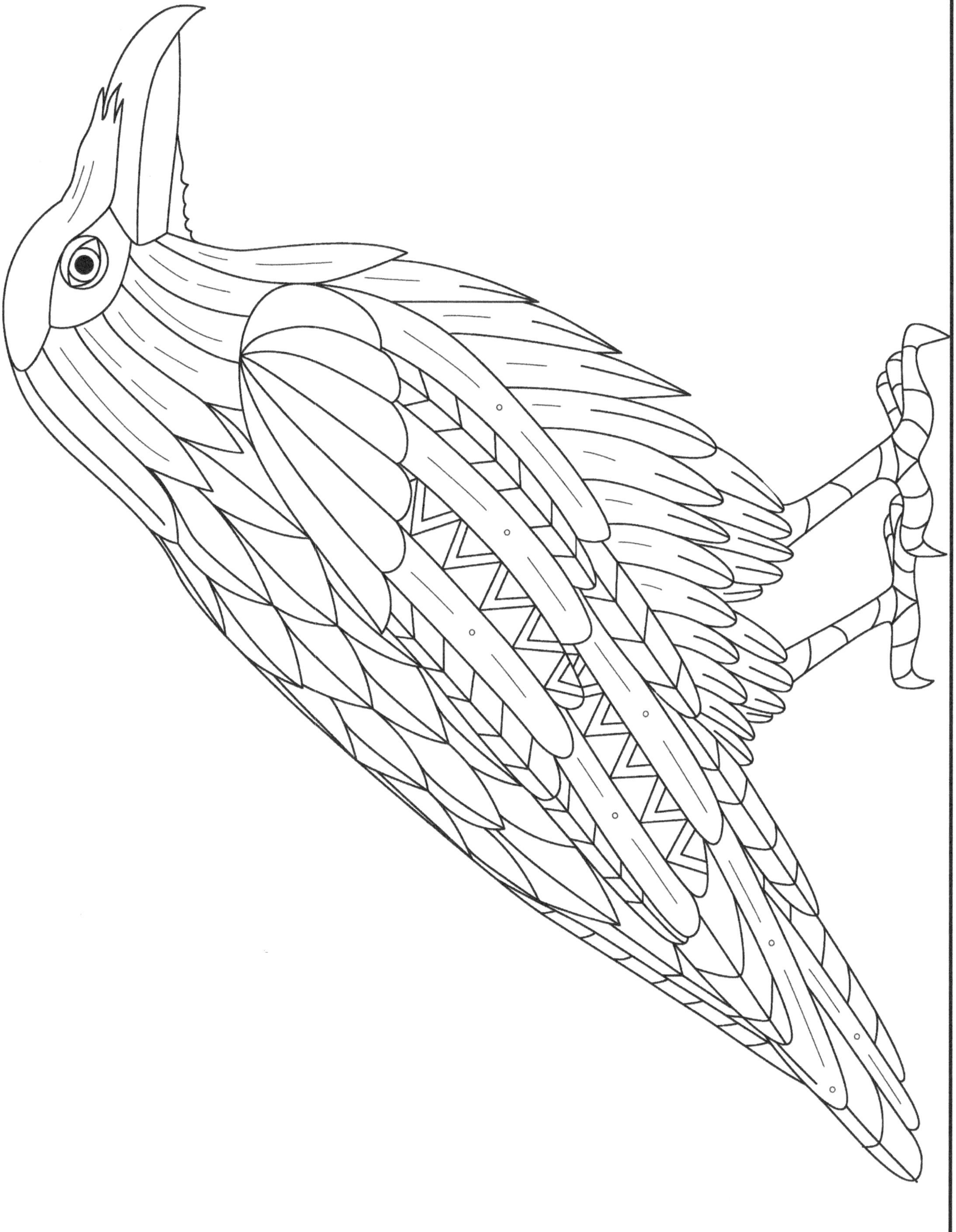

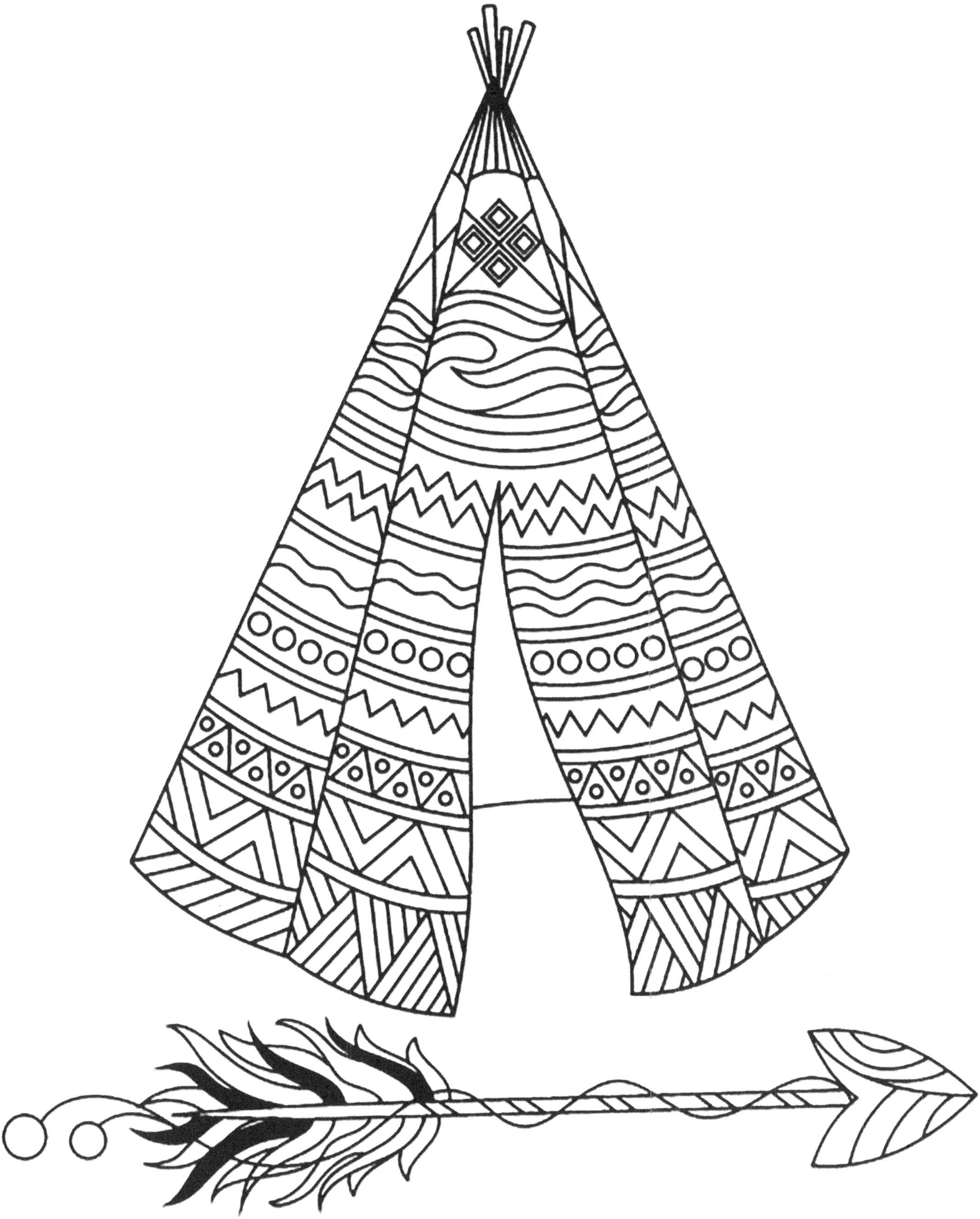

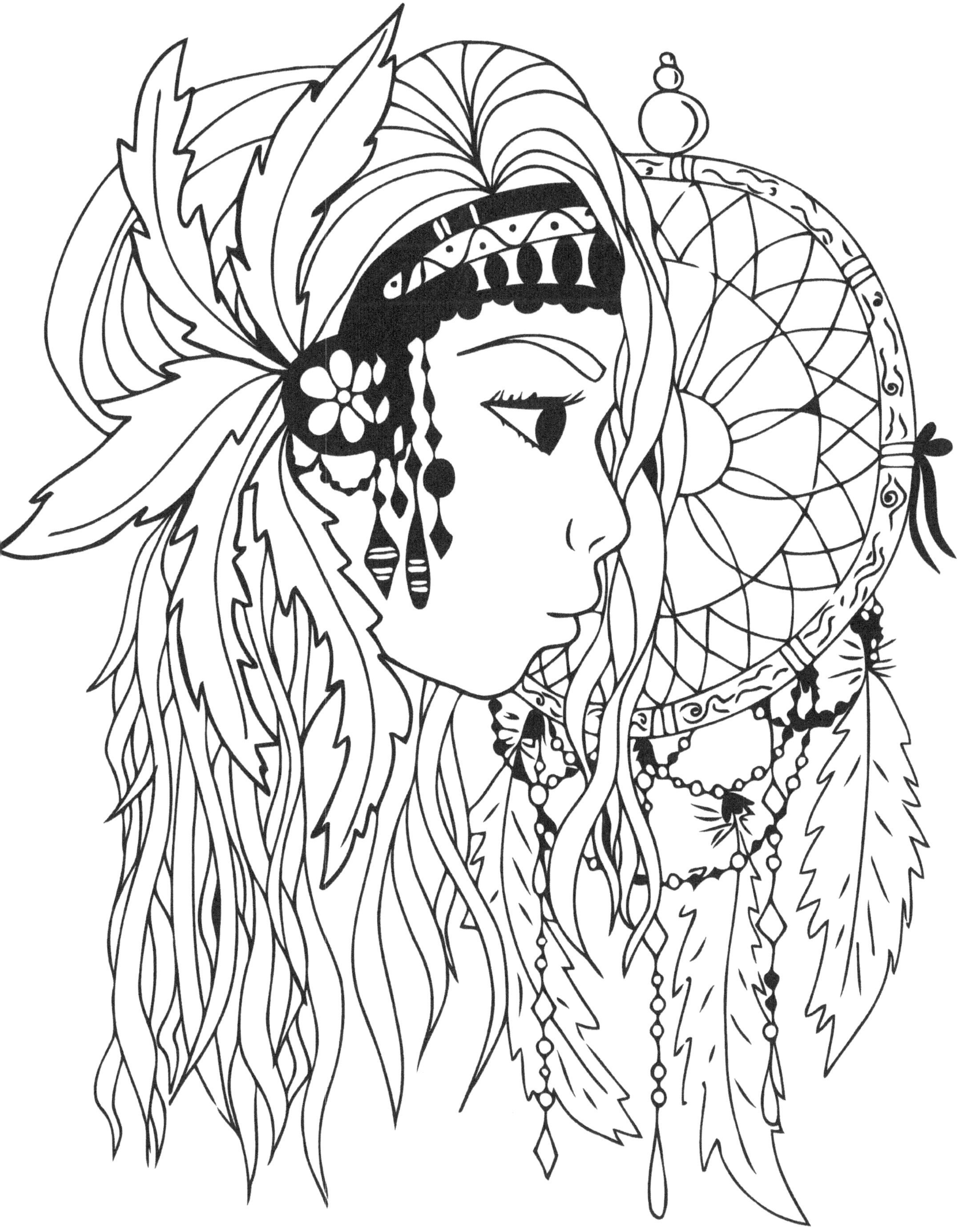

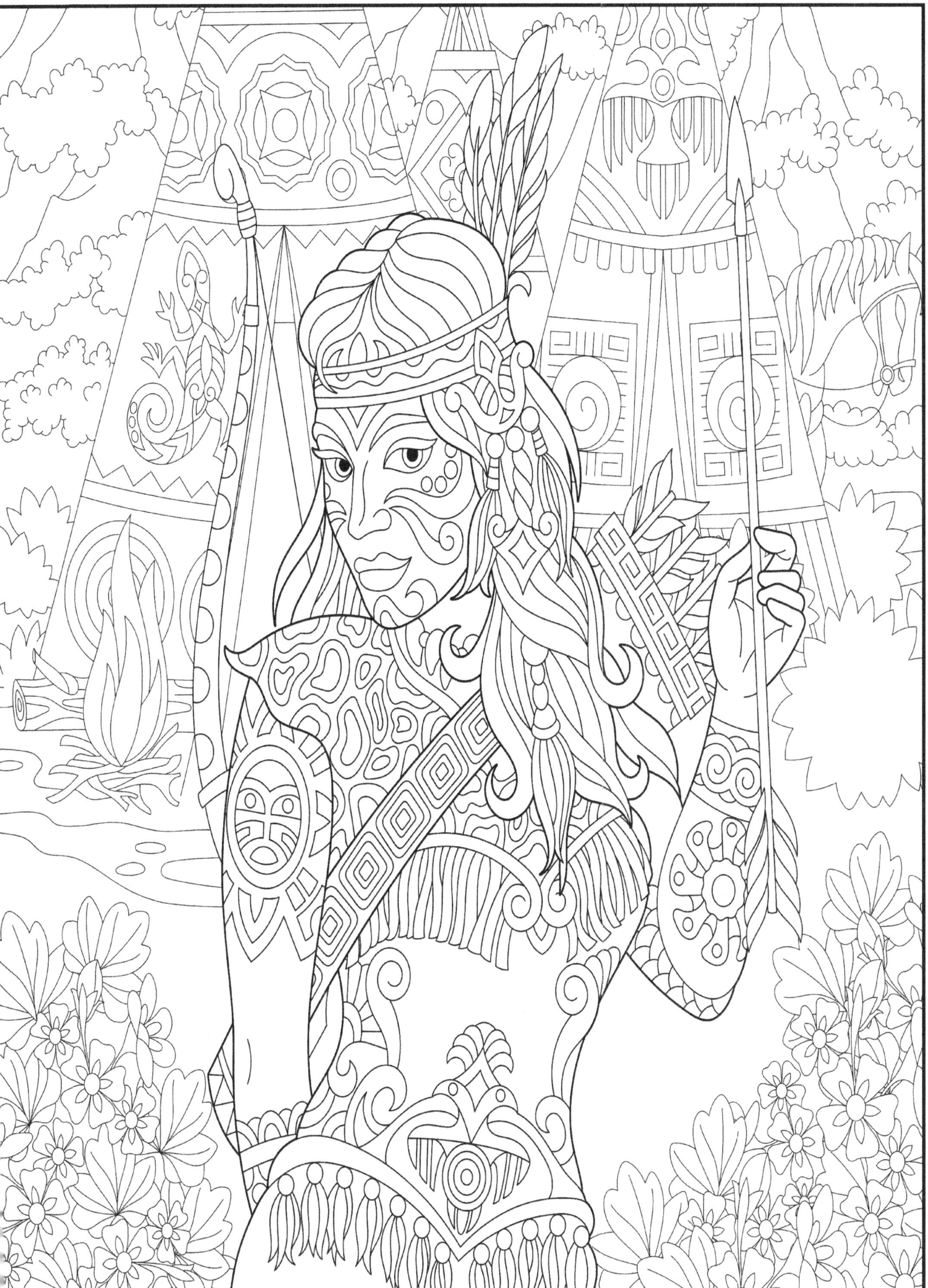

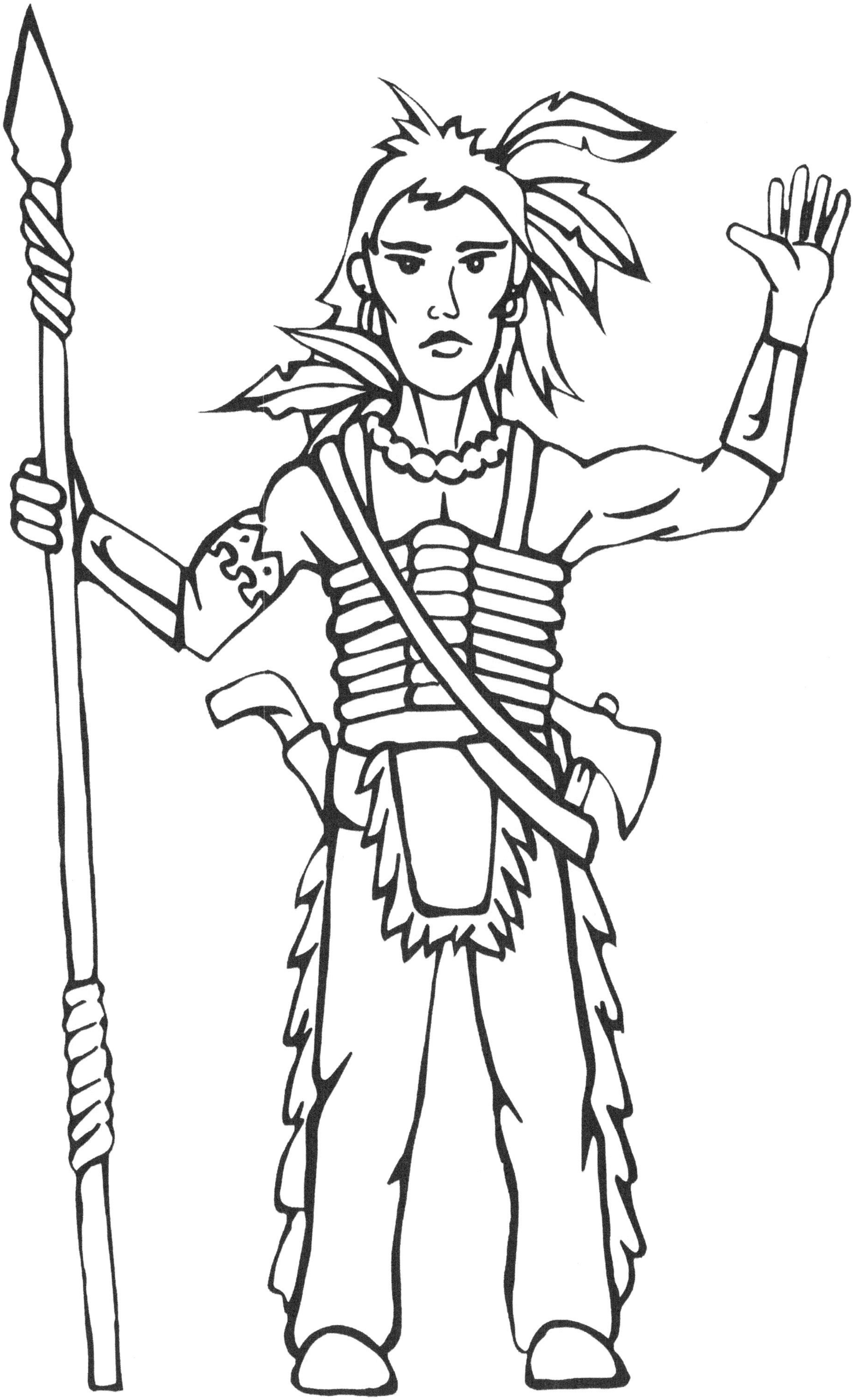

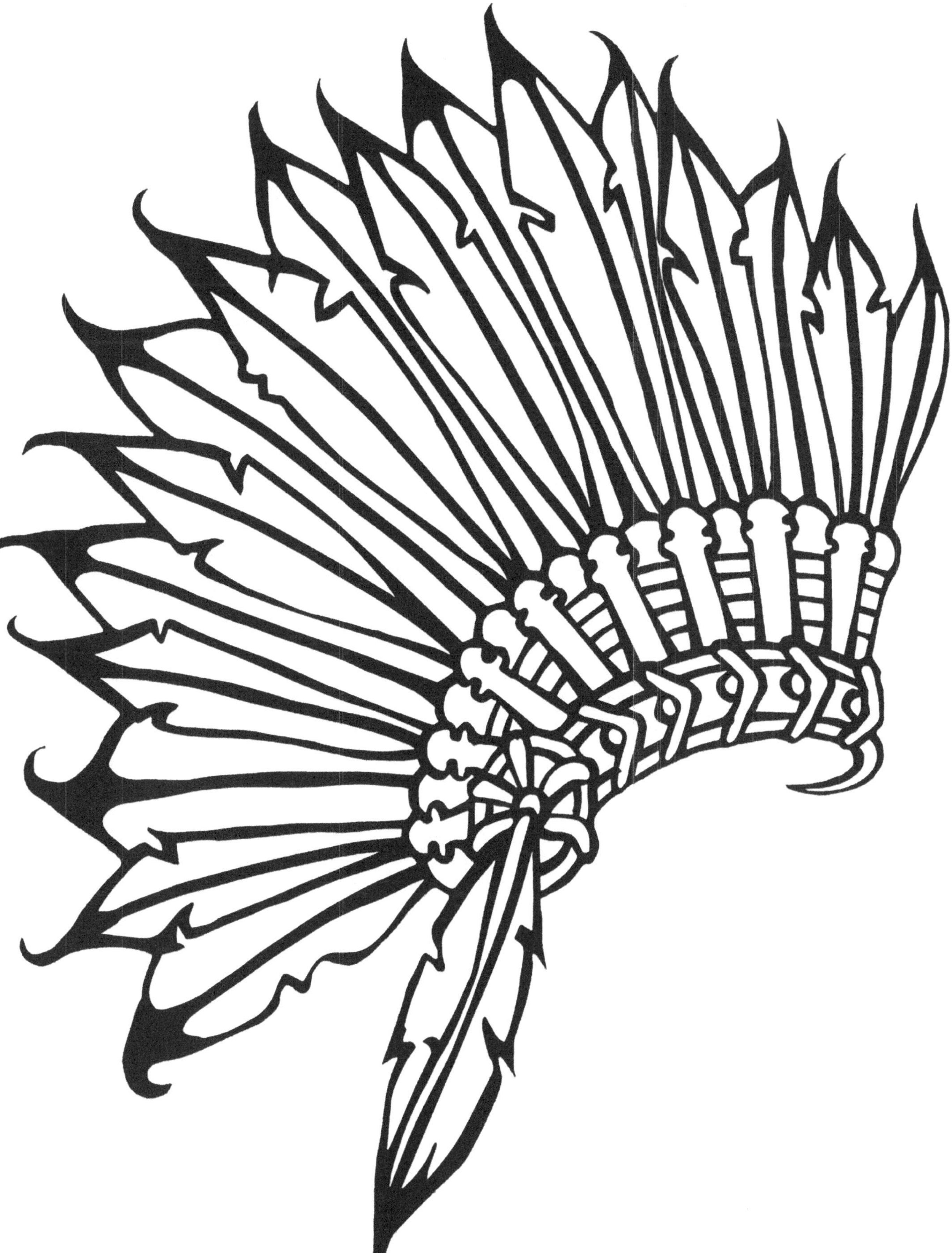

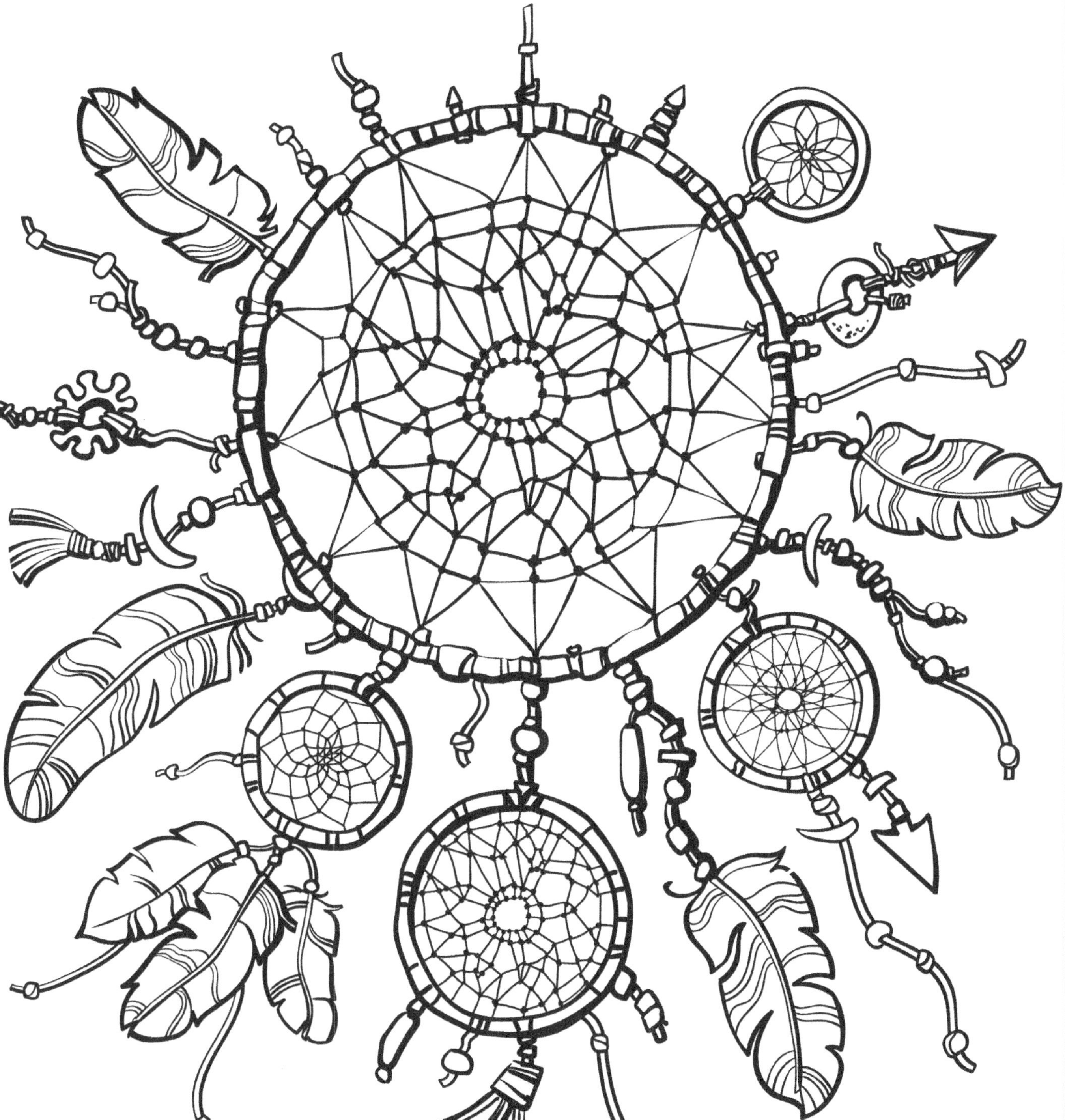

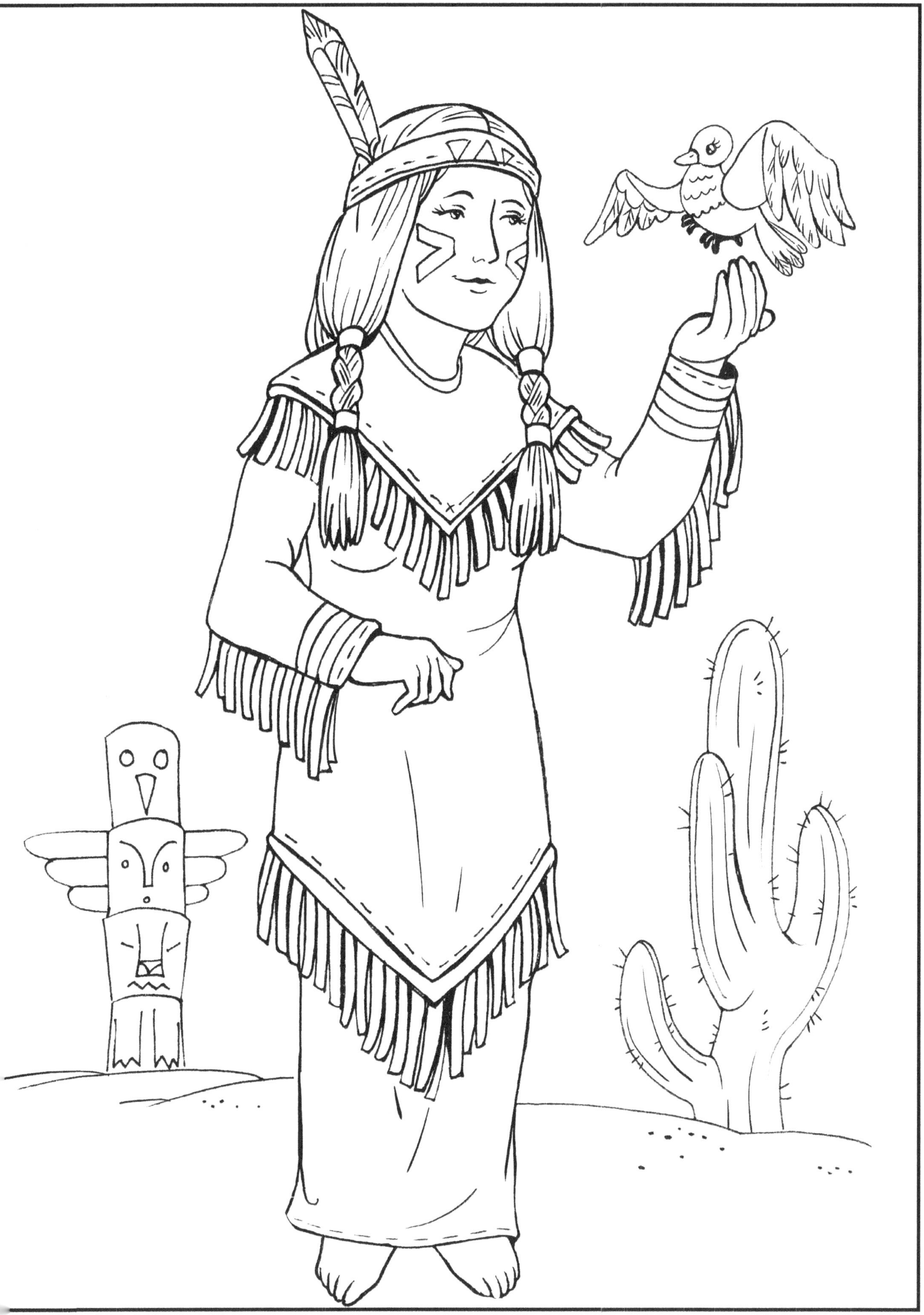

Made in the USA
Las Vegas, NV
01 May 2023

71382382R00070